The Photo Student Handbook

The Photo Student Handbook is a collection of short, easy-to-read chapters filled with expert advice on enhancing image-making skills and launching a career as a professional photographer.

Designed to help students grow beyond the technical aspects of photography, this book presents a variety of methods and strategies proven to strengthen visual awareness, engage creative thinking, and deepen the conceptual aspects of image-making. Topics include how to:

- improve the ability to see actively
- understand light as a main character
- cultivate a creative mind
- make a standout portfolio
- unpack critical theory
- find and develop a creative voice.

Packed with valuable tips, insights, and advice from over a hundred instructors, professionals, senior students, and experts, this book is engineered to help instructors guide students step-by-step through the methods and strategies needed to achieve creative success both in the classroom and the real world.

This book is ideal for intermediate- and advanced-level photography students and instructors alike. Visit the accompanying website www.photostudent.net for extra chapters, exercises, quizzes, and more.

Garin Horner is an award-winning educator, photographer, and author. He is the Director of the Adrian College Center for Effective Teaching and Vice-Chair and Secretary for the Midwest Chapter of the Society for Photographic Education. His previous works include *The Photography Teacher's Handbook* and *Teaching Photography*, 2nd edition.

The Photo Student Handbook

Essential Advice on Learning Photography and Launching Your Career Path

Garin Horner

Routledge
Taylor & Francis Group
NEW YORK AND LONDON

First published 2022
by Routledge
605 Third Avenue, New York, NY 10158

and by Routledge
2 Park Square, Milton Park, Abingdon, Oxon, OX14 4RN

Routledge is an imprint of the Taylor & Francis Group, an informa business

Library of Congress Cataloging-in-Publication Data
Names: Horner, Garin, author.
Title: The photo student handbook: essential advice on learning photography and launching your career path / Garin Horner.
Description: New York, NY: Routledge, 2021. | Includes bibliographical references and index.
Identifiers: LCCN 2021005995 | ISBN 9780367618162 (hardback) | ISBN 9780367618148 (paperback) | ISBN 9781003106685 (ebook)
Subjects: LCSH: Photography--Study and teaching. | Photography--Technique. | Photography--Vocational guidance.
Classification: LCC TR161 .H673 2021 | DDC 770.76--dc23
LC record available at https://lccn.loc.gov/2021005995

ISBN: 9780367618162 (hbk)
ISBN: 9780367618148 (pbk)
ISBN: 9781003106685 (ebk)

DOI: 10.4324/9781003106685

Typeset in Bembo
by Deanta Global Publishing Services, Chennai, India

Access the Companion Website: www.photostudent.net

Thank you

This book would not have been possible without the feedback, contributions, and advice from lots of people in my personal learning network and my creative support network, all to whom I am grateful. Thank you to student editors Olivia Vasquez and Rylee Meyer, to research assistants Katie Bellaire and Baylee Spangler, and to readers and contributors Dr. Carissa Massey, Professor Rob Dickes, Professor Brittni Collins, and Professor Mariah Postlewait. These students, colleagues, and friends were generously supportive with timely encouragement and insightful critiques. Also, my heartfelt thank you goes out to the many people who provided inspiring quotes, peer reviewers, and to my editor at Routledge, Alyssa Turner. I'm thankful that we all had the opportunity to work together and to reach our goal, to create a teaching and learning tool that can help students reach their goals.

Contents

Part 1
Explore

1

This Book's Audience

Students and Instructors

This book was written for two audiences: intermediate- to advanced-level photography students and their instructors. *The Photo Student Handbook* (*TPSH*) is designed as an essential guide for learners who want to take their photography practice to a level beyond a basic technical understanding. It is a collection of short, easy-to-read chapters filled with expert advice on how to enhance one's image-making skills. *TPSH* takes a unique approach. It is meant to help students excel in their photography education by providing a variety of methods and strategies that have been proven to strengthen visual awareness, engage creative thinking, and deepen the conceptual aspects of image-making. Combined with the guidance of photo instructors, the approaches in this handbook will help students avoid pitfalls that can slow progress and drag down grades.

FOR STUDENTS

This book delivers valuable tips and insights from over a hundred instructors, professionals, senior students, and experts. In these chapters you will discover thousands of years of combined knowledge, experience, and advice. All this is compiled into a single book, designed to be your helpful companion as you encounter ideas that promote personal and conceptual growth in your

10.4324/9781003106685-1

photography practice. In every section there are opportunities to expand your understanding and appreciation for photography by exploring how your ideas fit within the continuum of the photo-historical timeline.

This book was written for any student that believes photography is an important part of their life and will continue to play an important role in their future. At the same time, *TPSH* will guide you toward your own unique approach that will become the foundation for an individual photographic style. With that style, you can capitalize on applying your skills, abilities, and knowledge as part of a future career.

TPSH is intended to support/enhance the course design and teaching methods of your instructor. For example, when instructors provide learning opportunities, this book offers strategies to help you take full advantage of those learning opportunities. In these chapters there are innovative solutions to the challenges that can arise in your photography practice. If you want to heighten your creative abilities, find a path in photography, and improve the quality of your portfolio, then continue reading.

This book is intended for students who want to learn how to:

1. Use photographic tools to translate creative ideas and perceptions into photographic images.
2. Prepare for a fulfilling career that includes photography.
3. Discover a personal, unique photographic style or creative voice.
4. Use proven methods to enhance perception and visual awareness.
5. Make steady progress toward achieving higher grades.
6. Develop the confidence needed to take creative risks, while understanding why risks are important for artistic growth.
7. Apply expert advice on how to achieve your creative and academic goals.
8. Produce a standout portfolio, and more.

In addition, this book can relieve stress and anxiety by helping learners feel more prepared for the expectations of a rigorous photo program. In every curriculum there is a lot of information that's critical for success. *TPSH* was written to make sure readers receive the information needed to successfully integrate the advice of experts into an effective photography learning experience.

The first piece of advice is that, before reading, glance at each chapter title and ask, "Why should I care about this?" Ask, "What does this have to do with my life?" Keep these two questions at the forefront of your mind to prepare for learning. For instance, when an instructor says, "Today we are going to learn about proper exposure," you should ask these two questions. If you are learning about RAW files, color management, contemporary photographers, or critical theory, start with these questions. The reason for this is that, if you understand why you're learning something, the knowledge will become more meaningful. You will be more willing and motivated to retain what is learned and be able to integrate that knowledge into your understanding. Instructors should provide a little learning incentive by giving their perspective on why this information matters.

FOR PHOTO INSTRUCTORS, PROFESSORS, AND TEACHERS

The Photo Student Handbook is designed as a personal teaching assistant. The purposes of its contents are to:

1. Introduce a series of intermediate and advanced concepts to students outside the classroom.
2. Help make time available in class to engage students with hands-on active learning.
3. Present instructors with topics for in-class and outside-of-class discussion.
4. Provide a conceptual framework that students can use to gauge their progress.

It doesn't matter whether teaching happens in a classroom or online – this collection of valuable topics provides an opportunity to take student achievement to the next level. By delivering this learning material outside of class, instructors can spend more time with students interacting and actively engaging in course content. *TPSH* offers possibilities for instructors to select and integrate any or all of these ideas into their individual curriculums.

The number-one purpose of this book is to support student learning. It encourages students to thoughtfully respond and apply what they are learning. It encourages them to explore the depths of their own creative minds as they become more engaged with the class. With chapters on cultivating creativity, planning and executing assignments, tips for unpacking critical theory, and making a standout portfolio, students can use the book throughout several years of courses and academic levels. It also turns students' attention toward thinking about the career potential of photography.

There is also a comprehensive www.photostudent.net website that offers students and instructors a wide variety of resources that includes an extensive list of historical and contemporary photographers, a photo reading list, learning exercises, printable study guides, quizzes, four extra chapters, and much more. The website's Chapter 34 is a Level Up Guide, dedicated to providing a series of defined, scaffolded levels that help students recognize how every level of learning is important for future learning. Terms like "emerging" and "masterful" describe levels of experience that coincide with attaining a sequence of ascending stages of experiential knowledge that reach toward photographic mastery. This is one of the many learning tools designed to help students conceptualize where they are on a scale of hypothetical learning levels and what they have to look forward to when learning in higher levels.

TPSH works well as a companion to *The Photography Teacher's Handbook: Practical Methods for Engaging Students in the Flipped Classroom*. The teaching methods in *The Photography Teacher's Handbook* complement the learning practices in this book. *TPSH* is also an effective companion to most conventional textbooks or to online resources that deliver instruction on the technical aspects of photography. *TPSH* can also be used as a stand-alone resource in the classroom and when teaching courses online.

Photo educators, please note that the content in this text is based on key predictors for student success, such as motivation, engagement with course content, time management, preparation, participation, and the belief in one's own ability to succeed.[1] Also included are methods for applying current research on how the brain learns and how it generates creative ideas. This text also incorporates Arthur L. Costa and Bena Kallick's "Habits of Mind,"[2] along with learning methods that will complement the teaching strategies discussed in *The Photography Teacher's Handbook*.

2

How to Use this Book

Advice on Taking Advice

This chapter is about how to get the most out of this book and provides tips on how to apply the advice you will find throughout these pages. For example, before you can unlock the valuable information contained here, decide how you will read this book. If the book is required for a class, then you will read pages as assigned by your instructor. They will choose which topics and reading sequence best support the course content. Or, if you are a proactive student, then you might want to start reading chapters that interest you most, so you can enhance your class learning experience right now!

You could study the book cover to cover and highlight the points you think will be most helpful in the near future. Then, as the semester goes on, it will be easy to refer to new topics as they come up. You could also read sections on demand, as the topics become more important. For instance, if you need to boost your creative concepts, you can read Chapters 14 to 18. If you aren't focusing on your career at the moment, then save those topics for later. You will find that the book is designed for a long-term education. This means that there are tips and advice that you can refer back to and use, throughout your entire photography curriculum. How you read the book is based on your course, the advice of your instructor, and your purpose.

As you make your way through the book, you will gain a deeper, more critical understanding of photography. You will also see how being an image-maker can benefit your life. You will learn essential information about how your brain works during the creative image-making process and how to use that knowledge to your benefit. You will discover what kind of photographer you

DOI: 10.4324/9781003106685-2

are and how that recognition can awaken your individual, unique photographic style. You will also learn what it means to be a successful student photographer. With this book, and the guidance of your instructors, you'll go through a 10-step growth cycle, where you will:

1. Consider the purpose, direction, and benefits of your photography practice.
2. Develop your ability to intentionally see, with a sense of awareness and insight.
3. Use those newfound skills to look at and analyze photographs.
4. Make images based on new understandings.
5. Receive helpful feedback from your instructors, classmates, and people in your photographic community.
6. Reflect on what you learn from step 5.
7. Embrace new ways of thinking about photography, especially your own.
8. Contemplate where your photography fits into the conversation of all photography.
9. Apply realizations to revise/upgrade your approach.
10. Start the cycle again.

These 10 steps will help deliver success in your photo classes by supporting your photography practice. They will bring your attention to an ongoing cycle of creative growth, all while laying the foundation for a fulfilling career plan for after college.

To read and learn effectively, you need to *see*, *record*, *remember*, and *restate* what you learned. To help with that process, here are three useful tips:

1. Keep your phone close at hand, as you will need the Internet. There are two groups of names that appear in the book: those who offer words of advice for your learning; and photographers whose images are given as prime examples for the topics discussed. Go online and do a Google Images search for the names of each photographer you encounter. This will give you a visual reference (*see*) and a context for what you are learning.
2. Take notes. Either underline, highlight, and write in this book, or keep a notebook where you write down (*record*) any information you don't want to forget. Think of recording as saving information as a back-up hard drive for your brain.
3. Try to remember what you just read, and write a few lines to help you *remember* and *restate* what you just learned.

It's beneficial for your growth as an image-maker to look closely at a wide range of photographers' work. To get the most out of the *historical and contemporary* image-makers incorporated throughout this book, go to www.photostudent.net > Resources > TPSH Photographers and download the check-off sheet. When you go online and look at a photographer's work, put a check in the box next to their name. You can also make a brief note about the work to help you make an association between the photographer's name and their photos.

Now that you have a basic understanding about what this book can offer, let's consider how you can get the most out of your learning experience. Each chapter contains lots of advice.

To gain the most from any advice, do an experiment and try it out. Put it to the test. If you benefit from it, great – try another piece of advice. If that second recommendation produces positive results, try another. If you reach a point where you feel confident that by acting on the guidance in this book you will gain an advantage with your photography practice, then wonderful! When you feel convinced that what you read will help, this will motivate you to take the leap from reading the advice to actually applying it. Trust your intuition, but also watch for proven results.

The suggestions in this handbook are selected to help you in lots of ways to become a more knowledgeable, purposeful, thoughtful, and conscious student photographer. At the same time, the advice you read will support your path to becoming a masterful image-maker. This book is an invitation to be part of a dynamic collaboration with the people that provided recommendations and your photo instructors. Your instructors are the keys to your success, because they will help you understand, integrate, and internalize all the new things you'll learn. As part of your learning experience, they will also provide their expertise, knowledge, and connections to the larger photography community.

Your instructors are in a unique position to guide you, because they are familiar with how your work has evolved over time. They know the struggles, stumbling blocks, and successes you have achieved throughout your photography curriculum. Because of this they are able to lead you through exercises that can result in artistic, technical, and even personal growth. Your instructors can offer guidance that is timely, helpful, usable, and specific to your needs because they understand your work and your goals.

Part of getting the most out of your college experience is taking the time to connect with your teachers, instructors, and professors so you can build strong professional relationships. Make it a point to cultivate these relationships. Find one or two trusted instructors that can serve as mentors. A mentor is someone who has achieved a great deal of success because of their level of experience and mastery. This person also sees your potential as an image-maker and is willing to help you achieve the heights of that potential.

Mentors come in all shapes, sizes, and qualities, but a true mentor will feel personally invested in your educational experience and growth. They will provide expert guidance when you need it, open doors when you are ready to walk through, encourage you, and even challenge you to take creative risks that can move you beyond your creative comfort zone and to the next level.

Start now by taking advantage of office hours. Look for instructors you connect with and feel most comfortable with. Find someone who is interested in your work and seems to understand who you are and what you want out of life.

Have some face-to-face conversations. Begin a dialogue by stopping by with some questions about a topic you are learning in class, like an assignment or a reading. Find their office, step through the doorway, and say, "Hey, I need your advice …" They will be glad you stopped by. And so will you.

With or without a mentor, you can do this. You can learn how to use a camera, organize your compositions, and translate your ideas into images. Everything you have learned and experienced up to this point contributes in some way to the future learning you will need for your photography practice. Most photographers, including your instructors, have been exactly where you are right now, working to overcome the obstacles that come up throughout an academic program. Those photographers have also found learning to be a rewarding, gratifying experience. It's something they care about. You can do the same by not giving up on your daily practice of making photographs – especially when it's hard. Remember that you have access to support systems (discussed in Chapter 9) to help you feel connected and to help build the confidence needed to accomplish your creative goals. Use every resource available.

One more tip for using this book. On the website you will find an Appendix under the Resources heading in the main menu. This Appendix contains a series of handy check-off sheets that will keep you organized and on track. The lists are set up in a top-to-bottom series to help you at a glance to prioritize activities, tasks, topics, and practices during your learning experience in photography. Think of each list as a map of important destinations on the path of your photo-educational journey. You will be able to see where you have been, where you are, and where you are headed by plotting your path toward the highest level of photographic accomplishment.

Check-off sheets can also help you learn about your creative purpose. They can reveal subjects that inform and motivate your photographic practice. Organized lists can point out where your attention is going, topics you are attracted to, why and how you photograph the things that show up in your images. All of this information helps you become more visually literate. In other words, the things you learn about your own photography can make you a more insightful photographer.

You will notice that in the Appendix the pdf files have been provided both individually and in one file that contains all the sheets in a printable group. You can print the resource sheets separately as you need them or, if it makes for a more efficient workflow, you can print all the check-off sheets at one time. After you print the sheets, organize them in a three-ring binder. Keep your binder beside you when you read, so you will be able to keep track of the photographers you discover as you make your way through the next chapters of the book.

3

10 Things Your Instructors Want You to Know

Your instructors have a major influence on the success of your photographic studies. In many ways they work for you, not in an employer-employee relationship. Rather, they work for you by designing courses, assignments, and other tools to engage you and motivate you to learn. Throughout your curriculum, instructors help you build skills and abilities as you learn how to use your camera, look at images, critique, and excel to attain higher levels of mastery. With the long-term guidance of your instructors, you will gradually feel more empowered to pursue your creative ideas. As you gain confidence, instructors will encourage you to challenge yourself. The goal is that you become a self-motivated self-learner who finds success with accomplishing your image-making goals. As Socrates once said, "Teachers help you not by giving you something, but by drawing out what is already in you." When it comes down to it, your instructors may work hard for you, but to succeed it is you who must work for them!

To help you achieve those goals, here are 10 things your instructors want you to know.

1. *Your ideas are important.* Part of your photography practice is to embrace a willingness for world-discovery, life-discovery, and self-discovery. When you begin learning photography, your instructors don't expect your ideas to be fully developed. What they are hoping for is that your concepts and curiosity will evolve steadily over your time in the curriculum.

DOI: 10.4324/9781003106685-3

None of your ideas are bad ideas if they are something you care about or find interesting. Your instructors may help nurture those ideas so they can develop, grow, expand, and evolve into new ideas that lead you toward further discovery. Your instructors know that your ideas will take you somewhere rewarding if you stay on the path and keep making photos.

2. *The only kind of learning is self-learning.* It's your instructor's job to deconstruct information and deliver it in small, sequential chunks that help you learn and understand. Your instructors will create circumstances where you can use your new knowledge to gain more experiences. They will guide you and offer feedback on your progress so that you can move to the next levels of learning. What they can't do is make you learn. What you learn is completely dependent upon your level of engagement.

   Learning is an active principle. It can be compared to planting a seed. Nobody can make a seed grow. You can put it in nutritious soil, give it plenty of water and light, but all the hard work of growing must be done by the seed. Real learning, like the seed, can only happen when you take advantage of the nurturing resources and valuable learning opportunities your instructor and program offer.
3. *You are the only person that can make your photos!* Nobody is as uniquely qualified to make your style of photography as you! Since photography is a subjective, personal expression, only you can make the photographs that express your ideas, perspectives, and mindset, all in your unique voice. It may take some practice before you are able to recognize your distinctive photographic voice, but it will happen if you stay focused on taking pictures. No matter what, keep making photos.
4. *You deserve all the enjoyment, enrichment, and creative frustration that being a photographer offers.* These experiences will take you further in your creative work than any amount of talent, knowledge, or expensive equipment. The only thing that matters is that you are a determined student with a goal to become a more masterful photographer tomorrow than you are today. Being a persistent, committed learner will bring a sense of direction and purpose. At the end of the day, persistence overcomes all learning obstacles.
5. *Your photo instructors are not your friends or your peers.* You may be on a first-name basis with your instructors, but know that your relationship with them is different than a friendship. It's more like a professional working relationship. Instructors, especially your mentors, are willing to support you and advocate for you, but that it isn't dependent on you being their friend. Instructors have sustained their passion for photography over many years and have successfully risen through the levels of both the academic system and the photography world. They have found success. That fact puts them much higher on the scale of mastery than you. In this way, they are not your equals.

That being said, get to know your instructors. Establish a professional relationship with the people who will be giving you advice about your future and writing letters of recommendation. Make an effort to impress them. And don't be offended if they decline to be your friend or follow you on social media.

6. *People judge you by how you communicate.* Therefore, it is important to understand how to use the language of photography. Each photo-language is specific to the category of photography you are studying. For example, photographic terminology is distinctly different between topics such as DSLR cameras, critique, and critical theory. Start building your vocabulary and practice writing about your photography.
7. *Give yourself permission to experiment, even though the end result may likely be unsuccessful.* The experience you gain from exploring and failing can lead to successes you might otherwise not achieve. Failing is an important part of the learning process. Failures can lead you to a sense of purpose and help you find a direction for your work.

   Beginning photographers tend to go for the low-hanging fruit. These are the most common subjects you can find on your campus. For instance, a shutter-speed assignment compels lots of students to photograph water running out of their kitchen or bathroom faucets. This subject matter is common, comfortable, quick, easy, and safe. But it isn't interesting. Think of something else to photograph, something that's fascinating and original. Don't be afraid to try something crazy! Google Philippe Halsman's photo of Surrealist artist Salvador Dalí, *Dali Atomicus,* which features flying cats, splashing water, and Dalí floating in midair! Like Halsman, take some creative risks.
8. *Take on a leadership role by making class-time a dynamic, learning-rich experience.* Take control over your learning process by being a proactive self-learner. For example, if you want to learn how to create a quick collection in Adobe Lightroom, jump right on YouTube and find a tutorial by Lightroom experts Julieanne Kost, Laura Shoe, or Victoria Brampton. Then, offer to show your classmates how to make a quick collection. This self-directed style of learning is practice for what you will have to do after college, when your instructors aren't around to teach you. You might as well take ownership of your learning now.
9. *Make photography one of your superpowers!* If you feel like you aren't creative or don't have any natural talent for photography, you should know that these qualities can be learned, developed, and practiced. You can strengthen the quality of your photography by practicing in a deliberate way. For instance, if you don't understand composition, try following the rules of composition and learn what they have to teach. As you integrate that learning into your practice, composition will become intuitive.

   Try some of the creativity exercises and don't be surprised when your brain starts generating new ideas. The more successful your photos become, the more your confidence and abilities will grow. Again, remember that persistence and determination will always prevail over a lack of talent, skill, or creative abilities. The secret to success in photography is to make photos every day for a month. On the last day, choose your favorite 10 and get critical feedback. Try again for another month and, again, get feedback. Keep doing this monthly until you reach your goal.

10. *Content is king*! Instructors may give you a grading rubric that tells you which aspects of an assignment you should focus on. Beyond what is on the rubric, your instructor expects you to really think about and be deliberate with the subject matter you choose to photograph. Your instructors offer you the freedom to choose what you want to photograph and how you want to photograph it.

    With this freedom comes the expectation that you will consider the content of your photos and think about how the content you select is meaningful and/or interesting. It's kind of like being a creative chef. You want to invent a dish you will love, and that can't happen unless you consider the quality of the ingredients. The kind of ingredients and proportions are what makes the dish either a culinary tour de force or something that is unpalatable. Consider the content of your work!

4

10 Things Your Instructors Don't Tell You

There are some things your instructors don't tell you. Maybe they think you already know. Maybe they think that, if you don't know, you will find out from other students. In any case, here are 10 tips you *must* know.

1. *You could be more concerned with impressing your instructors.* The good news is it takes so little to impress them! Come to class on time, be curious about the homework, ask some good questions, and plan how you intend to make interesting images for your assignments – and before you go out and make photos. Impressing your instructor can bring lots of advantages that support your learning objectives and your photography practice. It can also play a beneficial role when you launch your career path. If your instructors believe you're genuinely interested in photography and that your work is impressive, it could raise the quality of future recommendations.

   Making an impression on your instructors is a great way to start building an after-college professional network. If you aim to impress, this raises the energy behind your degree of effort, which can result in higher grades (because you are working harder and learning). Plus, you'll be able to ask for those letters of recommendation or those instructors' names as references. You may also gain access to your instructors' network of connections in the photography world. These are all very valuable assets!

DOI: 10.4324/9781003106685-4

2. *Procrastination can be a powerful method for boosting creativity.* Studies have shown that procrastination can boost creative potential. Adam Grant, an organizational psychologist, conducted studies that show moderate procrastinators to be more creative than people who plan ahead and get projects done ahead of time. Grant believes that, because procrastinators have time to "incubate" ideas, it gives them "time to consider divergent ideas, to think in nonlinear ways, to make unexpected leaps."[3] Given the nature of the creative mind, it can take time for the storm to gather before the lightning will strike!
3. *For creative people, final grades aren't as important as you think.* In many cases, grades are secondary to a standout portfolio. And sometimes grades can be the third most important part of college – behind the portfolio and professional relationships you have with people in your field, your instructors, and classmates.
4. *Many of the photographs you make aren't that interesting.* Don't be discouraged! Most of the images that people make aren't successful. The thing that makes your uninteresting photos so important is that capturing those compositions is necessary for the growth of your photographic abilities. There is an old saying that goes, "Not all acorns that fall will produce an oak tree." Hundreds, if not thousands, of acorns have to fall before one emerges as a towering success! Photography is the same. You need to make those hundreds or thousands of unsuccessful photos to arrive at those images you want to put in your portfolio. Being faithful to your practice is an important part of the process, which leads to achieving images of excellence and discovering your voice as a photographer. So, never be disheartened by boring, uninspired photos, because they are just the acorns that pave the road that leads to success.
5. *Unless you are in a commercial photo program, the purpose of college (and photo courses) isn't necessarily to get a job.* The purpose of academic opportunities is to provide learning experiences that inspire you to think. Your college curriculum, which includes photography, helps you refine the ability to think critically while accelerating your creative maturation process. An essential part of that process is also to teach you how to learn. Self-directed learning will be your lifeline after college. If you plan on continuing your photo practice and getting a job using photography, then you have to be able to learn and adapt to a constantly evolving professional field.

   College also helps you develop:

   - a complex understanding of the world you live in and your relationship to it
   - a wealth of marketable skills needed for higher-paying jobs
   - an important network of lifelong connections with others (classmates, instructors, and professionals)

- a high level of personal responsibility that is required for a successful life
- the realization that what you learned can contribute to a more meaningful, purposeful life.

6. *College instructors commonly assume that the main reason you are in college is because you want to learn.* They hope this is true. It's likely their teaching approach is based on this assumption. It would help your instructors to know that, for some students, *learning* isn't their primary motivation for being in college. Students may be in college because it's the next stage of life, the step that comes between high school and a real-world job. Students could be in college because, if they want to level up to the next stage of life, this is what they have to do.

   Knowing what your instructors think can help you navigate your classes. You can use this information to impress your instructors by showing them that you really *are* interested in what they have to teach. Show them evidence that you *are* learning. For example, if you're writing a major paper for a class other than a photo class, make an accompanying photo-essay of images and turn it in with your paper. Also, show your photo instructors what you are doing, and you may impress more than one instructor at the same time!
7. *Some instructors prefer you not to see their work.* They don't come out and say it, but they don't want you to identify their work as being an example of "good" photography. They don't want you to emulate what you see, believing you'll get an A if your work looks like theirs. There is a real possibility that students may emulate the work of their instructors. Instead of imitating their work, most instructors would rather help you continue down the path of your own stylistic discovery.
8. *Opinions are limited.* When your photo instructors make suggestions, remember that these are just opinions. An instructor's opinion may be intelligent, insightful, and thoughtful, but it could conflict directly with another instructor's feedback. It could also clash with your purpose. Ultimately, you have to decide what parts of your instructors' opinions you can use and which parts to discard. Being able to sort through all the feedback is part of the maturation process of a student photographer.
9. *There is no such thing as a good or bad photograph.* Beginning students commonly ask two questions: "What is the difference between a good and a bad photo?" and "How do I make a good photo?" Instructors tend to shy away from answering these questions, even though they come from a student's desire to get a good grade and to take impressive images. Students sometimes ask such questions because they want to meet or exceed an instructor's expectations. Lots of instructors use them as learning opportunities by turning them back for their students to answer, as they can lead to engaging class discussions about what it is that separates

a good photo from a bad one. If you're in a beginning photo class where no one has asked either of these questions, maybe *you* should. Also, take a look at www.photostudent.net> Resources > Chapter 33 Is This Photo Good or Bad?

10. *There can be a lot of* chance *involved in photography.* Sometimes photographing is like going fishing. You take your camera for a walk, look around while being hypervigilant, and hope to stumble across something that will catch your attention. There are so many unknowns to consider. For example, you have to find a subject that is worthy of photographing, the lighting has to be right, and it all has to happen in the limited time you have allotted for getting your assignment finished. Unless you are lucky, and can find something interesting to stand in front of, you might have to take a different approach.

Part 2
Discover

5

Introduction to Photography and Why It Matters

> As we strive in our expectations for photographs to be truthful, to be factual, to be truth-tellers, evidentiary records, documentary makers, memory containers, windows to the world, or artistic objects, questions arise as to what photography is, what it does and, more importantly, what is it that photographs fail to do? While photography has seemingly always suffered from an identity crisis (Is it art or documentary? Is it a commercial tool or a social record?), it is a crisis that might encourage rather than disappoint, inspire rather than defeat.
>
> (Natalya Lusty and Donna West Brett)[4]

This chapter explores photography's ability to stimulate your visual and intellectual mind in ways that help you understand your world in new, remarkable ways! Still-frame images have the potential to show you unnoticed aspects of the world around you and even within yourself. They can teach the photographer and the viewer how to see and find meaning in the world.

By refining your ability to see, you can discover the ways photography reveals new realms full of interesting questions about *how* we observe and *what* we perceive. Author Susan Sontag said that "The painter constructs, the photographer discloses."[5] Photography's disclosures invite us to examine, think, relate, and imagine. It's an extraordinary art form that investigates important aspects of what it means to be human. It invites you to benefit from the insights that photography offers, as you learn to observe and decode the significance in

10.4324/9781003106685-5

what you see. And, in doing so, you may be inspired to express that meaningfulness in your own photographs.

Meaningfulness in photography can be understood through its product, the photograph, which not only records aspects of the photographer's experience but can produce an experience in the viewer. Photographs provide a kind of vicarious experience, but they can also provide a direct, firsthand experience. For example, think of holding a wood and gold metal frame containing a daguerreotype portrait from 1845. The object is a historical artifact, and that alone provides an experiential connection to the past, regardless of what was recorded in the photograph!

Professors Rebekah Modrak and Bill Anthes point out in their book *Reframing Photography* that photography is

> about actions involving looking. It's the act of reproducing an image an endless number of times. It's about questions of truth and authenticity. It's about pausing something that has life and movement so that we can watch it when it's still. It's about creating movement through fixed images. It's about the play of light and shadow. It's about finding photography in architecture and landscape, in design, in science, in everyday acts, and in making connections with the larger world.[6]

Photography introduces us to the common, the uncommon, the familiar and the unfamiliar.

Most of us will never have the opportunity to see in person the many things depicted in photos. We rely on images to bring the world and the universe to our eyes. Through images we can relate to unfamiliar subjects, as though we were at the scene as an observer, looking through the viewfinder at the instant the image was captured. It is a limited perspective but can offer a more enriching experience for those who know how to look. For instance, if you only see a photo as the subject portrayed on its surface, then you will be limited to a secondhand experience. But, if you look at the colors, composition, timing, angle of view, lighting, and the perspective of the photographer in relationship to the subject, then you can have a more direct, meaningful experience of what is happening in the image.

Photo curator Marvin Heiferman said that

> Photographs don't only show us things, they do things. They engage us optically, neurologically, intellectually, emotionally, viscerally, physically. They demand our scrutiny and interpretation. Photographs seduce and motivate us; they promote ideas, embed values, and shape public opinion. We look at certain photographs because they calm or excite us. Others solve problems or create them, empower or demean us. Photographs may foster empathy but can be equally effective at distancing us from whatever they depict.[7]

What a photograph can do is understood through its relationship between the unique way a photographer portrays the subject and how the viewer is able to receive and interpret its story.

Photography is a profound art form, yet most people misunderstand what it is and can be. For many, photography is the act of thumbing open a camera app, aiming, and pressing a big dot on a touchscreen. Everyone who has a phone is to some degree connected to photography, even if its purpose is simply to share images with their friends. But this is only the tip of the photography iceberg. Philip-Lorca DiCorcia once said: "Photography is a foreign language everyone thinks he speaks."[8] What DiCorcia is getting at is that snapping photos with a phone doesn't mean you understand the expressive power an image can have or the vast potential photography has to communicate your experience of living in this world.

The camera can become an extension of your creative ideas, offering the opportunity to actively observe and experience life in a deliberate way. Ralph Hattersley affirms that photography inspires a sense of purpose and that "We are making photographs to understand what our lives mean to us."[9] At its most fundamental level, photography can be seen as a tool for connecting with the world in front of your eyes. With such a tool you can turn the focus inward or outward, toward the complexities of your own mind or toward your relationship to the world you live in.

Photography is a method for describing your ideas, your mission, opinions, observations, questions, and the aspects of life you are interested in. In this way it's related to philosophy, because it provides a way for you to explore the "fundamental questions about existence, knowledge, values, reason, mind, and language."[10] Throughout the photographic process there are many chances to entertain your curiosity, to investigate, clarify thoughts, make statements, and ask questions about life, death, and beyond.

Photographer Jennifer Garza-Cuen sees "photography as a way to fill us with wonder, make us think, question or open dialogue."[11] That dialogue could be with your viewers or it could be an intimate conversation between you and your photographic images. Image-making can have an impact on your life at any point throughout the sequential steps of your workflow, as listed below:

1. Learn to actively see.
2. Develop creative concepts and/or follow your intuition.
3. Make photographs.
4. Study how to perceive and find meaning within images.
5. Think about and consider the significance of photos.
6. Talk about images.
7. Read other people's ideas about photography.
8. Write your own thoughts and observations about photos.
9. Refine ways of seeing, making, and thinking about photography.
10. Apply what you learn to develop new creative concepts.

Your instructor will guide you through all the above steps and help you integrate that knowledge into your practice. The goal is that you eventually come to realize, through direct experience, how comprehensive and consequential photography can be. Make it a goal to learn the importance of photography through the direct experience of study, analysis, and discussion of the many meaningful aspects of images.

One of the ways photography is important is that it allows you to capture a series of ongoing events that happen across a period of time. A camera's shutter is like a Pause button on events that are constantly changing. In other words, photos let us catch glimpses of moments within the flow of time by freezing instances, when it appears time has stopped and all things are permanently motionless. The camera captures the fleeting scene as it rushes by the closing window of opportunity!

Images capture and reveal minute details of a scene that you couldn't see with your eyes. In fact, by zooming in on a high-resolution digital image, you will discover details that you wouldn't otherwise know existed! Photos reveal obvious visual information that's hidden in plain sight. Because the eyes overlook most of what is seen, many visual elements are simply unnoticeable at first glance.

This recognition that photos capture things we can't see was made very early on, when photography was discovered. Even with the photographic technology of the mid-1800s, William Henry Fox Talbot said of his own images that,

> In examining photographic pictures of a certain degree of perfection, the use of a large lens is recommended, such as elderly persons frequently employ in reading. This magnifies the objects two or three times, and often discloses a multitude of minute details, which were previously unobserved and unsuspected. It frequently happens, moreover – and this is one of the charms of photography – that the operator himself discovers on examination, perhaps long afterwards, that he has depicted many things he had no notion of at the time. Sometimes inscriptions and dates are found upon the buildings, or printed placards most irrelevant, are discovered upon their walls: sometimes a distant dial-plate is seen, and upon it – unconsciously recorded – the hour of the day at which the view was taken.[12]

If you are perceptive enough, you can decode the evidence in a photo and derive meaning from what you see. In several fields of photography, like photojournalism, the image serves as truthful evidence. The image implies that what appears in the photo exists or existed. Photos inform about the subject matter and the context in which they were made. Images may hold clues about when and where they were created. There may even be evidence that reveals the maker of the photo.

At the same time, photography is important because of its ability to simultaneously capture a scene as it appears, while also conveying how the photographer interpreted the story it reveals. The photograph is a thin plane of space, a boundary between the life experience of the photographer and the reflections of the outer world.

When everything comes together in a perfect instant, your resulting photo can teach you about how your intuition and your life experiences work together to express something about your vision of the scene. The resulting photo is unique, because of the way you saw it, from your perspective during that now-extinct moment of time. The images can even bring to light evidence about your psychological, emotional, and/or intellectual reactions to the subjects you photograph.

Consider all of that which remains unseen, cropped out of the image. For instance, photography is a subtractive art. When you crop in on a scene with your viewfinder, you remove, or subtract, it from its context. Your frame excludes much more from the scene than the small box the composition presents. By using a specific vantage point, you choose to crop out the greater majority of all that's visible around you. It's a deliberate choice and leads the viewer to conclude that all other vantage points would have produced a less adequate image, a photo that could not express what you saw in the scene.

A photo may imply that the scene in the composition continues forever outside the boundaries of the frame, while in reality, just outside the borderline, there may be studio lights, gobos, the edges of the background, and assorted equipment. For example, there is more to William Eggleston's photo of a red room, *Greenwood, Mississippi, 1973*, than meets the eye. When you look at Eggleston's photo, it shows how the image was made – you'll see all the things that exist just outside the frame (look it up for yourself). Seeing how the scene was constructed completely changes the way you look at and understand the photo.

Photography represents a series of choices. You make a conscious choice about when you will push the trigger release. In doing so, the viewer can assume that the instants before and after the capture were less likely to produce the intended image. Even so, those moments are still meaningful, because in every photo there is an

> Implication of [not only] what was left outside of the frame; what happened before this moment and what might happen next; and most fascinating of all, the viewers themselves, mirrored by their very individuated interpretations, filtered through their own cultural and historical background.[13]

Every photograph has much to teach and it's up to the viewer to mine the depths of its content.

When you look into the viewfinder, your eye may not notice the many visual relationships formed by the elements in the scene. You might not see all the details included in the composition. But you can perceive the overall visual qualities, intuiting whether or not the scene presents a holistic, unified photographic composition. If all the conditions are right, and you anticipate capturing a compelling image, your brain will give a little nudge that tells you to push the shutter release.

Looking through the viewfinder can make you aware of how your vantage point affects the way elements are arranged in a scene. You learn how composing a photo is a way to convey meaning. Composition is used to show the viewer many things, such as how to look at the subject in the photo, the order of importance, and how visual relationships support the story within the photo.

When the human brain perceives these relationships, it interprets shapes, colors, and forms so it can derive meaning from what it sees. Stephen Shore said: "Photographers have to impose order, bring structure to what they photograph. It is inevitable. A photograph without structure is like a sentence without grammar—it is incomprehensible, even inconceivable."[14] Thus, photographic composition is a visual language that you need to learn and integrate into your photo practice before you can fully understand what you see.

As a viewer, use the visual evidence in the frame to interpret what you think is happening. Your brain will activate memories to formulate meaning based on what you see. Jonathan Bayer declares that photographs

> enter the realm of art because they invite the viewer to participate and to decipher them. They stimulate the mind, assault it, amuse it, set problems for it and give it the sublime satisfaction of coming up with its own answers. "Good" photographic images intrigue, present a mystery, or demand to be read. They are constructs of frustrations and ambiguities which force the viewer to actively interact with the photograph.[15]

Photography is important because it confronts the habitual, passive way of seeing the world and offers a chance to observe intentionally, dynamically, and actively. It teaches you to understand the act of seeing as a conscious, deliberate act. It's a manner of perceiving that recognizes everything that can be seen as being full of meaning. Jim Stone points out that

> No work of fiction, nothing in a personal fantasy, could be as endlessly compelling and fascinating as the real world around us. Photography's central role in our culture is the direct result of its power to describe that world. It is a visual medium whose most effective use emanates from direct experience.[16]

Photographs, especially of common subjects, bring focus back to the details we have overlooked a thousand times, because, as we go throughout our days, we largely miss most of what's around us. Images of these ordinary scenes bring attention back to a subject in a way that offers new clarity, all because the viewer is given an opportunity to see the subject from a perspective they have never seen it before. In this way, successful images elevate their subject's sense of importance so dramatically that observers are able to see these subjects anew.

Photography has the capacity to transform the way people see the world by informing, persuading, and making viewers feel roused to action. Photojournalism and photo activism certainly intend to use photographic imagery to awaken the viewer's sense of urgency. Their images bring awareness to the need for social, cultural, political, or personal change.

Effective images can bring awareness that translates directly into new ways of understanding, new ways of behaving, and possibly revolutionary acts that initiate change. Visual images are valuable in their ability to inform, teach, and persuade. During the Vietnam War, photos were used in the media to expose the horror and injustice that many North Americans didn't know was happening. That imagery turned many Americans against the war. Photographs became an important catalyst to convert apathy into a strong motivational force that got people off their couches to make phone calls, to join like-minded people of purpose, and protest until the United States left the war in 1975. Images have the power to initiate change by making viewers feel that what they see in photos matters to their lives.

Photography can facilitate the cultivation of self-awareness by gradually helping you learn about the motivations behind your image-making practice. Self-awareness is important because it can lead to an understanding of who you are and what you have to say. It exposes those things that you are most interested in, what you care about, what is important to you, what concerns you, and what excites you. "A photograph is not limited to what it exposes but can be limitless to what it reveals about you."[14] Those revelations can inspire you to express aspects of your life that are deeply important and meaningful to you. In your photography practice, you may come to recognize the people, places, and events that have had the most impact on the development of who you are as a person. When you understand these things about yourself, image-making can provide insights about where you instinctively point your camera.

Photography offers many choices for how to best express your interests, thoughts, and feelings. You could use straight photography, digital imaging, or multimedia. Your approach could be literal, metaphoric, symbolic, or poetic, whichever approach works best to describe those things you can see and even those things you can't. Jane Hirshfield, in her book *Ten Windows*, eloquently describes poetry in a way that also perfectly expresses the poetic approach to photography. In the quote below, you can easily replace every "poem" or "poetry" with the words "photograph" and "photography."

Hirschfield says that

> A mysterious quickening inhabits the depths of any good poem – protean, elusive, alive in its own right. The word "creative" shares its etymology with the word "creature," and carries a similar sense of breathing aliveness, of an active, fine-grained, and multicellular making. What is creative is rooted in growth and rising, in the bringing into existence a new and autonomous being. We feel something stir, shiver, swim its way into the world when a good poem opens its eyes. Poetry's work is not simply the

> recording of inner or outer perception; it makes by words and music new possibilities of perceiving. Distinctive realms appear to us when we look and hear by poem-light.[18]

Lastly, part of what photography is is an extensive commercial industry focused on providing images for clients that range from individuals to corporations. Though the competition is fierce, talented students can use their photography, business, and people skills either to make a career or to supplement a career. Photos created by commercial photographers don't tend to be as introspective or critical as those made by photo artists. Their intention is less about asking questions or investigating personal interests as it is about using creativity to meet client needs and expectations.

The scope of *what photography is* is vast and is not limited to the descriptions in this book. What you have read is an overview that hopefully expands your understanding about it. This chapter is intended to make you think, to ask questions, and seek out answers about how photography can become an important part of your life.

6

What Kind of Photographer Are You?

You might be the kind of photographer that likes to explore, to hunt for visual treasures, to seek out and photograph subjects that exist in the world. Or you may prefer to pre-conceptualize an approach, to make an idea real by fabricating some or all of the subject matter. This could be something as simple as rearranging elements in a scene or constructing elaborately staged, designed tableaus. Most photographers set out to discover something in the world, while others use their imagination to create and photograph the worlds of their imaginations. The following photographers have gone to great lengths to design and fabricate all the subjects they photograph: David Octavius Hill, Robert Adamson, Jeff Wall, Sandy Skoglund, Gregory Crewdson, Cindy Sherman, Bernard Faucon, and partners Lori Nix and Kathleen Gerber.

Everyone wants to know where they fit in, where they belong. This chapter will help you find out what kind of photographer you are and where you fit in. Chapter 6 is designed to provide an overview of the many kinds of photography that people practice out in the world. As you look through the categories below, you will hopefully find some approaches that appeal to you, that you feel you most connect with.

To begin, look within for what inspires and motivates you. Make a list of five topics in your life that you find most fascinating or are curious about. Once you have a basic idea about what your interests are, this chapter will help you discover how those interests are instrumental in defining your classification as a photographer.

DOI: 10.4324/9781003106685-6

Here are four motivational factors that likely play a part in what prompts you to pick up a camera and take photos.

1. Personal interest projects, sometimes called "passion projects."
2. Course assignments (which easily become personal interest projects).
3. The concept of a visual diary, research, or photo-sketchbook (on your phone?).
4. Photography that you do for others (as a volunteer or for payment).

When you look at the work of other photographers, what kinds of images, genres, or topics are you most attracted to? What kinds of subjects do you most enjoy photographing? If you can't narrow down an answer to this question, investigate the images you have already created to find clues. If most of the images you've made are unrelated – for example, you made some photos for assignments and others are snapshots on your phone – then maybe you haven't found a topic that you are passionate about.

If, after studying your photos you just can't find any commonalities among your favorites, then you could continue to experiment with many different subjects and approaches. Photograph some landscapes, make some portraits in natural light, cover a sports event, and go into a studio to build a still-life and light the scene. Use the list below as an inventory of possibilities for subject matter. Try to make a small portfolio of images for each of five or six categories and see which photos you most enjoyed making. Out of those photos, which ones are your favorites? The most important goal of this experiment is to discover which photos you feel are most meaningful to you. Your goals are to:

1. Discover subjects you are most interested in photographing.
2. Decide how you want to photograph those subjects.
3. Consider your approach (conceptual, intuitive, poetic, technical, shocking, or contemplative).

Find out what kind ofphotographer you are. You may feel compelled to highlight the way people live in the world, like Dorothea Lange. This genre is referred to as the "human condition." For Surrealists, like Salvador Dalí, Kyle Thompson, and Robert and Shana ParkeHarrison, dreams and nightmares provided potent material for their photographic artworks.

Technical photographers

> are the go-to people when you want advice on buying equipment and dealing with computer hardware or software problems. They are logical, analytical, realistic, and practical thinkers. They believe in order, pay attention to details, and like having control over all aspects of their work.[19]

Ansel Adams was certainly one of the most famous technical photographers. He even invented a technical process called the Zone System, so he could create images that more perfectly represented the way he pre-visualized his natural subjects.

Fine artists warn that aiming for technical perfection can put you in danger of making beautiful, but boring images. Sometimes imperfections can be important characteristics in a photo. As my grandfather once said, "Skill of hand will never make up for emptiness of heart." Still, there are lots of photographers that are able to use technique in a way that supports their purpose and story, while at the same time applying enough artistic qualities that their images come alive for the viewer.

If you are an image-maker who's intellectually inclined, who enjoys thinking, ideas, and theories, then a conceptual approach may interest you. Concept-centered photography begins with an idea and sets out to illustrate, ask questions about, or elaborate on that idea. Conceptual ideas could be portrayed as literal, metaphorical, or through symbolism. Identity, race, culture, and social justice are examples of topics that inspire conceptual photographers.

For example, Melissa Kreider is a social activist who advocates for victims of sexual and domestic assault. Kreider's photo series "Remnants" focuses on 12 instances of domestic and sexual assault in August 2015. As part of her activism, Kreider has collaborated with actress Mariska Hargitay, who plays a police officer on the television show *Law & Order: Special Victims Unit*, as collaboration is part of her conceptual approach. If you are interested, collaborations are another possible approach to photography.

Early in the history of photography, ideas around truth versus fiction arose as one of image-making's major topics. In 1840, Hippolyte Bayard portrayed himself as a drowned man. His photo served to illustrate his feelings of betrayal, despair, and dejection for being overlooked as an inventor of one of the first successful photographic processes. Soon after, viewers of the image were shocked to discover that Monsieur Bayard was actually still alive! The general public was confronted with the fact that photographs aren't necessarily evidence of reality.

Further examples of photo-historical conceptual photography can be found in the work of Robert Frank, Frans Lanting, Man Ray, David Bailey, and Robert Doisneau. A few contemporary examples, provided by LensCulture, include Marja Pirilä, Ali Mobasser, Daisuke Takakura, Chino Otsuka, Michael Somoroff, Jon Horvath, and Manuel Cosentino.

The majority of art, photography included, is created intuitively. Intuitive image-makers set out to take photos prepared only with their cameras and basic ideas for their approach. Instead of planning out their ideas and content, they remain open to the possibilities, without preconceived notions about specific goals. Intuitive photographers may also respond instinctively with how they use camera settings. Part of their method includes the belief that only finished images can reveal the photographer's purpose and a photo's meaning. Examples of this way of working can be found in the work of Mindy Véissid and Gregory Halpern.

Another option is the visually poetic approach in which photographs are used to refer to things you can't see, like emotions or spirituality. Examples can be found in the work of Luis González Palma, Manjari Sharma's "Darshan," Adi Nes, and Bill Viola. Photographers like Torsten Andreas Hoffmann, Jonathan Foust, Stephen Batchelor, and Jamie MacDonald also take a visually poetic approach. Poetic photographers may incorporate symbols and metaphors, so it helps if they have a grasp of visual literacy. Like written poetry, the visual language is used to point toward ideas and feelings without using imagery to illustrate them in a literal way.

If you think about it, anything your eyes can see (and even some things they can't) is a potential topic for photography. When choosing subject matter, make a point to use things, themes, or topics to which you have access. For example, if you want to photograph mountains but live in a place where there are none, then this isn't a practical subject to choose.

The list below doesn't include all possible reasons people make photos, but they are topics to consider. If you are still having a hard time deciding what interests you, start crossing off everything on the list below that doesn't seem appealing. What remains at the end could be potential material for your photo practice.

THE PURPOSE OF YOUR PHOTOGRAPHY

Think about the purpose for your images, what you want your photographs to do. The action you want your photos to perform can be intimately tied to your motivation for making photos. Images aren't passive reflections of the world – they illicit reactions. Remember: photos "do" things. Below are some reasons why photographers are motivated to make images. It's because they want the photographs to:

Advocate
Analyze
Argue
Arouse
Capture
Communicate
Connect
Contribute
Convince
Deceive
Declare
Decorate
Discuss
Document
Enlighten
Examine
Excite
Exhibit
Explore
Expose
Express
Formulate
Generate emotions
Give pleasure
Give understanding
Go viral
Identify
Incite
Inform
Inspire
Instruct
Interpret
Intimidate
Organize
Persuade
Prove
Publicize
Record
Remember
Report
Reveal
Sell
Share
Shock
Speak
Teach
Testify
Verify
Witness

Or as:

A project
Evidence
Reference
Illustration

SUBJECT MATTER

Here is a list of subject matter, themes, topics, and/or genres that are popular with photographers. On the website www.photostudent.net> Resources > Chapter 6 Examples you will find a copy of this list that includes some names of photographers who specialize in these topics/genres.

Animals (wildlife, pets, insects, fish, amphibians, etc.)
Cities
Color
Common, everyday objects
Controversial subjects
Cultural
Cultures
Family
Fine art
Food
History
Ideology
Landscapes (earth, water, fire, and sky)
LGBTQ+
Man-made structures
Memories
Nature/wildlife
New topography
Nighttime scenes
Nonconformity
Nude
Past, present, and future
People (yourself and others)
Philosophy
Plants (flowers, fruits, vegetables, trees, etc.)
Politics
Religion/spirituality
Rural
Science
Social resistance
Society
Stories (narrative)
Text with image
Travel
Wide variety of objects

NON-VISIBLE SUBJECTS

Aromas
Colors (also Interpreted in black and white)
Emotions (anger, joy, social anxiety, stress, etc.)
Fantasy
Flavors
Hopes, dreams, pleasures, and fears
Ideas
Identity
Imagination
Music
Physical sensations
Poetry
Psychological darkness
Sexual identity
Spirituality (religion, good vs. evil)
Tragedy
Your story

THE APPLICATION OF TECHNIQUE

Abstract (organic or geometric)
Analog film (35mm SLR, medium format, and large format)
Angles (eye level, worm's-eye view, bird's-eye view, or Dutch angle)
Aperture (selective depth of field)
Black and white
Clarity (Group *f*64 vs. pictorialism)
Collage
Color palette
Compare/contrast
Compositing (Photoshop)
Composition (use of negative space, rule of thirds, etc.)
Conceptual
Creative
Dark (horror)
Dark/bright (high key vs. low key)
Depth of field (selective focus)
Design oriented (lines, planes of color, textures, and patterns)
Digital (phone, mirrorless camera, or DSLR)
Focus (soft/sharp)
Framing (macro, close-up, wide shot, three-quarters shot, medium shot, or point of view/POV)
Hand color
High dynamic range (HDR)
Historic/alternative processes (gelatin silver, cyanotype, collotype, Van Dyke brown, and others)
Humor
Hybrid (scanning film negatives)
Hybrid processes (film with scanning to digital)
Illustration
Impressionistic
Juxtaposition
Large format
Lenses (normal, macro, telephoto, or zoom)
Light (quality, intensity, direction, and color)
Light painting
Lighting (natural, strobe, candle, or other)
Long exposure (night photography, panning, and use of neutral-density filters)
Medium format
Minimalism
Montage
Mood and atmosphere
Motion/movement (blur/freeze vs. handheld/tripod)
Multimedia (photography with other art forms)
Multimedia/video/graphics/drawing/painting
Multiple exposure (or image layering)
Nostalgia
On location (site-specific)
Panorama
Period (appears to be from a specific time in history)
Photo-essay
Photogram
Pinhole camera
Reflections (in water, windows, or mirrors)
Series
Shutter speed (time exposure, time lapse, long exposure, panning, fast exposure)
Silhouette/shadows
Single frame vs. diptych, triptych, and multi-frame presentation
Size of the final prints/presentation
Studio (studio lighting)
Surreal
Symbolism, metaphors, and analogies
Tilt shift (Lensbaby or large format camera)
Time exposure photography
Toy camera (Holga, Diana, etc.)
Typology
Ultra-high resolution
Zoom with your feet (physically move closer or farther away from the subject)

GENRES AND CAREER TOPICS (FINE ART AND PROFESSIONAL)

- Abstract
- Activism
- Adventure
- Advertising
- Aerial/drone
- Animal rights
- Architecture
- Astrophotography
- Automotive
- Baby
- Boudoir
- Candid
- Child
- City life
- Commercial
- Community outreach (PhotoVoice)
- Concert
- Diverse subjects
- Documentary
- Editorial
- Environmental
- Event
- Family
- Fashion
- Fine art
- Food
- Forensic (law enforcement)
- Glamor
- Head shot
- Landscape
- Lifestyle (events: weddings, bar mitzvahs, vacation, cruise ship)
- Medical
- Newborn (babies)
- Nude
- Sports
- Pets
- People (race, culture, the human condition)
- Photojournalist/news/AP/war correspondent
- Portrait (art/commercial)
- Product/tabletop
- Racial justice/equality
- Real estate
- Rural life
- Scientific (research, documentary, or illustration)
- Self-portrait (selfie)
- Senior (high school)
- Social justice
- Social media
- Sports
- Still-life
- Stock
- Street
- Tableau
- Travel
- Underwater
- Vernacular
- War/conflict
- Wedding
- Wildlife

PROFESSIONAL POSSIBILITIES

- Editorial (publications/online)
- Graphic design/web photography
- Photo critic/reviewer
- Photo curator (museum or gallery)
- Photo editor (post-production processing)
- Photo editor (work with content editors, creative directors, and social media managers)
- Photohistorian
- Professor/instructor
- Residencies (national parks and others)
- Sales (photo industry)
- Teacher (camps, art centers, or community programs)
- Teacher (HS)
- Teaching artist (K-12)
- Teaching assistant
- Volunteer/nonprofits
- Web designer (for photographers)
- Workshop leader
- Writer on photography (blogger, freelance, books)

Photographer Rick Sammon was determined to become a travel photographer. Rick worked a day job and considered his travel photography to be a serious hobby. Then one day he decided that, in order to take his dream to the next level and become a successful travel photographer, he had to do what travel photographers do. He bought a photo/travel vest, the equipment he needed to achieve his goals, and started taking the trips he could, within his means. Eventually he became the photographer he wanted to be. Now, he is an acclaimed travel photographer, teacher, and author of over 40 books![20]

Once you settle on a direction to take with your photography, you (like Rick) can set out on the path to become the photographer you want to be. Take an account of your skill level, knowledge, and quality of work, and guess where you would fall on a spectrum between amateur and highly skilled professional. Then, find out what you need to learn to move forward, to the next level.

Visit this book's website, and study the work of those photographers and the images that are part of your chosen genre. Learn about their paths to success. If they are alive, contact them and share your photography hopes and dreams with them. Ask them some questions about how they got where they are today. Thank them for their inspiration and ask for advice. With the help of your instructor and your CSN (creative support network), make a five-year plan and set goals for what you would need to do to accomplish those goals. Lots of photographers made and followed a plan for success, and you can, as well.

7

Your Photographic Voice

As an emerging photographer, it's important to recognize and develop your unique photographic style, which could also be referred to as your *voice*: "a unique and recognizable artistic style that is distinctly your own; your inspiration, your materials, techniques, themes and color palette all working together in a way that looks like it comes from you and no one else."[21] For example, when you look at photos by Samuel Fosso, Les Krims, and Deana Lawson, it's obvious which images belong to each of these photographers. Some day in the future, viewers may look at your photos and know, with some certainty, they were made by you.

Consider all the unique ways you express yourself. The way you talk, the topics you typically discuss, the clothes you choose to wear, the music you listen to, and the foods you like to eat are all ways you express your sense of individuality. All these things are extensions of your unique life experience, beliefs, physiological qualities, desires, view of the world, and your sense of identity. You are special in that there is no one like you. The way *you* make photographs in many respects relates directly to the distinctive way you live your life.

Finding your photographic style starts by closely looking at who you are, what you have to say, and how you prefer to say it. As a result, your photos will express these insights into who you are. Your photos tell viewers about the particular way you see and interpret the world. In other words, you communicate through your photographs by showing them interpretations of the world, in ways that only *you* see it. Unless you are a press photographer who strives to be

10.4324/9781003106685-7

objective, your creative practice should be to capture subjects, not as they are but how you understand or envision them to be.

In order to figure out who you are as a photographer, follow the trail of information that leads to the answer. Part of the evidence that points the way can be found in the many photos that you've already made. If you've made a collection of photographs over many years, there is nothing more valuable than studying how and why you captured those experiences and subjects. Establish an ongoing dialogue with your photos. Pay close attention to the images you most feel a connection with and figure out what they have to say and how they say it.

The theory is that your photos will show that you naturally, habitually choose subject matter that is most important to you. You will intentionally bring emphasis to the parts of the scenes that interest you most. If this is true, then the photos you examine will reveal where your photography is headed. The types of compositions you are attracted to can teach you how to solve the mystery of your photographic voice. This is an evolutionary learning exercise that leads you toward:

1. The discovery of subjects you are most interested in photographing.
2. Understanding the unique ways you prefer to photograph those subjects.
3. The breakthrough of recognizing the identifiable characteristics of your unique artistic style or voice.

Then, focus on qualities that describe who you are and what's meaningful to you. In lots of ways, your approach to photography, as mentioned above, is made up of how you see the world, your opinions, memories, emotions, and experiences. The people you have known, the places you've gone, and everything that happened in between your birth and this moment has shaped your preferences and interests. These things influence what you are most attracted to as subject matter. That includes the colors, shapes, composition, lighting (and much more) that you are partial to.

You may be the kind of photographer that likes to feature people in your photos or the type that doesn't. You might prefer black and white over color. Or, you could be the opposite. You could be one of those rare image-makers that is attracted to both. These individual preferences, habits, and characteristics are clues that provide useful information while you are trying to discover and develop your photographic voice.

Discover your style by performing these five activities:

1. Make lots of photographs.
2. Study those photos with mindfulness and curiosity.
3. Ask people in your CSN (creative support network) and PLN (personal learning network) to offer feedback on what they perceive regarding recurring themes, common visual elements, and shared subject matter.
4. Develop your level of self-awareness farther.

5. Compile and critically examine a collection of other people's photography with which you feel a connection.

It matters a lot how you carry out these five activities. Everything you need to discover your style is most likely hidden in your photos (it isn't actually hidden, it's just that you probably can't see it). Collect a group of your own favorite 20 photos. What makes you choose these photos as your favorites? Your answer is a helpful clue. It's hard for any photographer to look at their own photos objectively, but you will become more perceptive over time! The better you get at observing and visually deconstructing your work, the more insights you'll discover about your photographic voice.

We are habitual creatures and lean toward repeating visual features that seem familiar and make us feel pleased. Look for common threads that run through the group of photos you chose. You may notice that your horizon line tends to run through the center of the compositions. Or, you might see a lot of rural scenes in your backgrounds. Have some faith in what your observations can reveal to you.

In Angela Faris Belt's book *The Elements of Photography*, she talks about finding a *singular thread*. Faris Belt says that

> The thread is the singular overarching concept or theme that I believe runs throughout nearly every serious artist's work. Although you might have numerous portfolios, there is likely a single thematic thread running through all of them. If you're new to photography, then pay attention for your thread to emerge; the sooner you identify it, the sooner you'll be making the pictures that lie along the path of your real interests.[22]

If you are a novice photographer, you might not have any perceivable threads or patterns in your work. Your portfolio may consist of several different experimental approaches. Instead of expressing your photographic style, these images could be examples of your creative exploration, looking for subjects and ideas that interest you. If this describes you and your work, then you will need to make enough photos – a couple thousand, at least – to be able to narrow those down to 20 images that are your favorites.

You can also gain insights by getting helpful feedback. Some of the best comments you can get will come from the people in your CSN and PLN. These people understand what you are trying to accomplish with your work. They are the people most likely to point you in the right direction for achieving your goals. Their collective experience of working with you will help them make informed observations about how to best help you. Insights from your networks are invaluable.

A very perceptive reviewer will look for your photographic habits, behaviors, and the story your images reveal about you. Reviewers can sometimes see visual evidence that talks about your intentions and motivations, things that you may not be able to see. As someone once said, we tend to see other people's qualities with great clarity, while the person we see and understand least is our own self. The same can be said for our photographs.

Out of all these activities, developing self-awareness takes the most time. Self-awareness refers to your ability to look at yourself and your artwork in an objective way. In essence, it's the practice of closely examining your own interests, motivations, and reasons why you make photos. A person that is self-aware can clearly see the weaknesses and strengths in their work and use that knowledge to improve and grow. Reflect on how the things you believe influence your image-making and may therefore be reflected in your compositions.

To practice self-awareness, become a student of your own life. Learn from observing the connections that run through your life and your photography. Below are six questions that can help you become more introspective. Take as much time as you need to think about your answers.

1. What kind of subject matter are you most interested in photographing?
2. What aspects of your photography practice do you feel are most successful?
3. In what areas of your photography practice do you feel you could improve?
4. What qualities in your photography most express your habits, excitement, boredom, enthusiasm, unwillingness, apathy, interest, insight, and lack of insight about what you're doing?
5. What do you need to do to make your work more meaningful and important to you?
6. How can your work be more visually and intellectually exciting for you, especially while you are producing projects about the things that you're most interested in?

Becoming self-aware isn't a goal you can reach by the end of the semester or even within the time you get a degree. It's an ongoing process that unfolds for as long as you continue to self-examine. The process works best if you are proactive, determined to learn, and persistent with your goal to focus your attention on finding your creative voice. You can stay motivated because you know that every step in the growth of your self-awareness reveals hard-won revelations about you and your photographic style.

As you continue this long-term project, don't forget that your voice will never be set in stone. Your creative practice is an adaptable, evolving process. As you learn more about yourself, give yourself permission to change your mind about what interests you. Remain free to pursue novel techniques, innovative concepts, new subject matter, deeper learning, and fresh understandings.

Part of what keeps photography exciting is that you can, at any time, branch out and experiment in new creative territories, outside of what feels safe and familiar. Make part of your photographic identity the willingness to take some creative risks. Take the opportunity to discover that "your true creative voice might be just on the other side of your current comfort zone."[23]

In addition to the *six activities for discovering your photographic style* listed above, here are two additional methods that may help. The first is to find 20 to 30 pieces of other artists' work that inspire you or with which you feel a connection. Then, figure out what it is in their work that you find most alluring. Using the same investigative techniques you use to look at your own photos, observe the work of your favorite artistic creations. Mindfully identify elements that you are attracted to visually, emotionally, psychologically, or even spiritually.

You can choose artworks from any kind of medium – it doesn't have to be limited to photography. It doesn't even have to be specific artworks. It could be a genre of art. Maybe the Neoclassical or Romantic periods inspire you. Or, perhaps you love Surrealism. This activity is intended to help you discover the qualities that appeal to you in particular works or genres of art, and to think about how those qualities relate to the photographs that you make. Look for connections between what inspires you and the work you produce as an image-maker.

You may not find perceivable visual or conceptual connections between your inspirations and your own work. In that case, ask yourself, "Why not?" And, if not, try an experiment to incorporate five of those elements into your own work. See how this experiment can help bring your photography in line with your identity as a photographer. Maybe you are interested in studio portraiture while also being blown away by the high-contrast, hyper-detailed etchings of Albrecht Dürer. Or you find the collaged compositions of Robert Rauschenberg fascinating while focusing on landscapes as a subject matter. It could be that you are drawn to street photography and consider what it would look like if made with an Impressionistic approach. Or possibly you would like to focus on close-up photography that uses a futuristic style.

Photographer Joel-Peter Witkin uses Renaissance paintings and the work of historical photographers as inspiration for his own photography practice. Witkin uses painted backdrops and classical props to construct "macabre often grotesque scenes. Working in the vein of the earlier photographers Henry Peach Robinson and Oscar Gustave Rejlander, Witkin carefully builds scenes with cadavers, hermaphrodites, and dwarfs which introduce literary, religious, and art historical allusions."[24] The scenes are often recreations, with his stylistic twist on the original Renaissance artworks that inspired him. Witkin applies his unique approach, his voice to the recreations, making all his photography recognizable as *his* work.

The point isn't to copy the visual qualities of things you like. It's to experiment with a hybrid approach that can help you break new ground in ways that align your photo practice with your preferences, your photographic voice. As your photography starts to reflect aspects of your life, you could make new discoveries. The possibilities are endless. This creative exercise will produce results that are specific to what interests you most, how you interpret those interests, and who you are as a photographer.

Another suggestion is to design your own photo project based around a subject or concept that you want to photograph. Dream up a custom-made assignment that focuses on your interests. It's exactly the kind of assignment that you could get excited about! Take this opportunity to excel and make a group of images that you really want (or desire) to make. Ask your instructor what you would need to make this exciting, creative possibility a reality. Use what you learn with this assignment to confirm that only *you* are uniquely qualified to make photographs from your perspective, your vision. Once you find your voice, celebrate your discovery by picking up your camera and finding new opportunities to use it!

8

Find Your Audience

If it's important to you to be a visual artist, then it should also be important to be a *visible* artist. In other words, if you are a photographer you can probably assume people will see your images. Are you concerned with who will see the photos you make? Maybe you are like 1930s photographer John Turner, who didn't really care about viewers because he documented London for his own pleasure and enjoyment. Or, you could be like photojournalist Maggie Steber, who makes photos to inform viewers about important events happening around the world. You may identify with William Wegman, who targets an audience that loves dogs and has a sense of humor. Photographers have many purposes for making images and there is a wide spectrum between those that don't care if anyone sees their work and those that want everyone to see their photos.

Artist Barbara Kruger has a targeted audience for her work. Her photos focus on "cultural constructions of power, identity, consumerism, and sexuality,"[25] and some of her work is aimed directly at people in authority. You may decide that your photos are intended for the small audience of high-art culture. Andy Warhol or the Starn Twins made their fine art photography for that audience. The real question is: Who are the viewers that you think are most interested in seeing your work? Is the audience you imagine a lot like you, interested in things you like? Do they think like you? It could be that your intended audience is your photo classmates and your instructors. Or, it could be the students in all photo programs around the world. Or, maybe your work caters to a larger

DOI: 10.4324/9781003106685-8

academic community of students, instructors, like the members of an organization such as the Society for Photographic Education.

The instant you make a capture, someone will see it – even if it's just you, looking at a preview on your view screen. Hayes Gordon once said that "Amateur art is about self-expression – professional art is about communication."[26] In both instances, making photographs is a deliberate act that expresses a fact or describes an idea. Where there is expression, there is an audience. Expression is a statement that has meaning. It informs and tells some kind of story. An image communicates something about the experience of the photographer and describes how that experience relates to the subject matter.

An image, no matter what the subject, can elicit a response from a viewer. The photographer, the images they make, the scene, and the viewer become connected through a conversation that begins when an image is captured. To continue the conversation, you need to know who your audience is, who is most likely to respond.

Your first group of viewers is likely your instructors and classmates. They are your inner circle of supporters, the starting point for your larger audience. These people are with you on a daily basis and you have a shared history with them. They understand your work in the context of undergraduate or graduate studies and are likely to have an appreciation for what you produce. This group of people is sympathetic to your work because they are companions on your creative journey. They are the only ones that have an intimate understanding of your growth as a photographer.

The next circle out probably includes friends, family members, and others in your CSN. This group may not be able to see the depth and complexity of your work because of their limited experience and knowledge of art and photography. Even so, they are interested and want to support you.

The third circle audience is composed of people you don't know. These viewers are more objective because they don't know much, if anything, about you. They found some connection with your photography without being influenced by any historical knowledge or personal information. This is an important group of people, because they are fascinated only through a blind encounter with your work. They experience an aesthetic, emotional, or psychological connection with your images. In other words, your work communicates on some level to those viewers. These are the kind of people you should encourage to be part of your audience. Try to describe who these people are, because it will be helpful for your photography practice in the future.

Your audience is known by many names – for instance, fans, followers, admirers, and supporters. For professional photographers, they are also known as clients or customers. Whoever they are, it's valuable to know more about them as you work to establish a productive, mutually beneficial relationship. Here is how you can figure out who they are.

Circle whichever of the 24 categories that you feel best describes your target audience:

-Photo students
-Art students
-Professional photographers
-Amateur photographers
-Intermediate skills photographers
-Advanced skills photographers
-Clients
-Buyers
-Critics
-Artists
-Non-artists
-Students
-Professionals
-Gallery curators
-Museum curators
-Local viewers
-Regional viewers
-National viewers
-Online viewers
-International viewers
-Facebook followers
-Instagram followers
-Males, females, others
-18–25, 26–35, 36–45, 46–55, or older

Consider the best way to target your audience so you can start a dialogue. Based on your assumptions, consider where you will show your work so people can see it. You have so many choices when it comes to showing your images to the world. You aren't limited to putting framed photos on the walls of a traditional brick-and-mortar gallery, though this is a viable option. There may be more effective ways to get your work seen.

Physical spaces are still the standard for exhibitions, yet will always limit the number of viewers you can get to stand in front of your photos. Galleries and museums also offer very limited opportunities to meet interested viewers directly. Sometimes it's nice to have face-to-face conversations and get direct feedback through people's reactions to your images.

The gallery experience can have more impact for a viewer, because there is something special about standing in front of an actual print. The viewing experience of a print is very different from looking at a computer monitor. With a print, the photographer chooses a fixed scale for the photo on the wall. With the digital version, the size of the image is variable, depending on the viewing device. Plus, people tend to be more receptive and more willing to spend time looking when they've dedicated time to traveling to an exhibition venue for the purpose of seeing work on a gallery or museum wall. The viewing experience becomes an event. Part of the specialness of the event is the limited access to the viewing.

In terms of accessibility, the Internet will always win when competing against the foot traffic of a physical exhibition space! An effective and easy alternative to exhibiting in a gallery is to post your photos online so anyone with Internet access and a device can see them. Better yet, use every exhibition opportunity you can get, both on a gallery wall *and* a screen!

As an emerging photographer, one of the biggest obstacles you will face with building an audience online is that the Internet is overpopulated with everybody's photographs. All this visual clutter can make it hard for your potential audience to find you. Given this issue, try to increase your online presence by making a website that features your work. Also post images to online gallery sites. On those sites, highlight your web address, to drive traffic back to your website. Do some research to find online gallery sites that are free and have the highest visibility, and where you think it would be easiest for viewers to find your work.

Here are 25 platforms where you can connect with and grow your audience:

1. Your photo class
2. Your photo program
3. Your website
4. Online galleries
5. Facebook
6. Twitter
7. Vine
8. Instagram
9. Podcast
10. YouTube/Vimeo
11. A bricks-and-mortar gallery
12. Pop-up exhibitions (in physical spaces)
13. Your blog
14. Other people's blogs
15. Give an artist's talk
16. Email (start a list)
17. Printed marketing materials
18. Online publications
19. Printed publications
20. Publish a book (hard copy and digital)
21. Your e-newsletter
22. Photo-sharing websites (Shutterfly, Photobucket, Imgur, Flickr, etc.)
23. Word of mouth
24. Public presentations/discussions about your work
25. Presentations on your work at conferences.

Now that you have a list, rearrange it into a priority list – from what you can do right now to what seems least possible. Professional event and sports photographer Jeff Cable has a sizable Instagram audience, with almost 13,000 active followers, yet his number one source for reaching clients is word of mouth! Jeff's lesson is: don't underestimate the word of mouth as a way to connect with your audience! With a worldwide reach, the great majority of Jeff's business success comes from a network of people who talk to each other and rave about his work.[27]

Once someone contacts you, you can start to build on the relationship. Build on initial contacts and stay in touch. Ask the members of your audience if they would like to receive news about your photography practice. If the answer is yes, give them your web address, connect with them on Instagram, and get their email address. Periodically share news, stories about your photos, or what is on the horizon (once a month, every other month, or four times a year). Blogger Kevin Chung said that you should

> Talk about your life and experiences and how they relate to your work. Talk about how your audience can relate to your work. Become a helpful and important part of their lives. When you build a connection with your audience instead of blasting them with messages that scream "Look at me!" you are strengthening your bond and becoming more likable. People want to help those they like.[28]

You may find it beneficial to offer incentives to bring people into your viewer circle, like giveaways. In 2018, outdoor photographer Travis Burke offered to give away his van, plus $6,000 of photo equipment. Burke asked his audience to tell him how winning would change their life.[29] Photographer Mikey Huff won! Your giveaway could be something less extravagant. If someone connects with you, send them an inexpensive yet personal giveaway like a limited-edition signed postcard featuring one of your photos. Or, offer them a small signed print.

Your goals:

1. Connect with your audience.
2. Guide your audience back to your website.
3. Start collecting an email list.
4. Build your relationship (I will explain why in a minute).

Your website, email communication, and word of mouth will be the three most effective ways to grow a relationship with your audience. Nonetheless, social media followers can become strong viewers if you keep them engaged over time. Photographer Dzvonko Petrovski offers some good advice when he says:

> Your social media accounts don't have to be filled with just the awesome pictures you are taking. That alone can make your audience feel a tad distanced from you, which is why behind the scenes photos and videos are really powerful in making the audience feel closer to you. When you show people the way you work, you are also putting a face to the person (in this case, you) – it simply looks more personal. That way, by showing the amount of work and skill required to capture photographs like that, paired with the personality and face behind the images, amplified by the friendly tone and engaging posts, you have a great formula for increasing and keeping your audience happy.[30]

Petrovski's advice parallels ideas to incorporate into your artist statement (discussed in Chapter 25), where people become interested to learn about you and your artistic process.

When you make photos, you might imagine how you would like your audience to respond. The reality is that you can never control or know exactly how viewers will react: "The audience interprets meaning, events, intention, and receives the work through the filter of their own experiences and associations. And that's one thing we cannot control. What is communicated and what is understood can be polar opposites."[31]

For example, photographer Barbara Nitke made a series of images that featured actors on the sets of pornographic movies. Some viewers may find her photos shocking. Others might think they're interesting from a sociological perspective. Still some viewers will find them aesthetically and conceptually alluring. These differences are embodied in a theory called the "intentional fallacy," which states that viewers are unpredictable and won't necessarily react to or interpret a photograph the way the photographer intended it to be understood. Each viewer sees through the lenses of their own life experiences, attitudes, and state of mind. As such, they will respond with their own unique interpretations and perspectives.

Another good reason for gathering an audience is that viewers can potentially provide helpful feedback on your work. They can also spark new ideas or help you see your work in new ways. Although general online comments can be empty of usable information, if you are lucky you might get positive reinforcement and encouragement from knowledgeable photographers. Positive feedback can be incredibly inspiring, especially when it comes from someone you hold in high regard.

Online viewers, especially the ones whose opinions you value and respect, become part of your PLN (personal learning network). Think of your audience as another kind of network, a go-to resource for creative collaboration. From time to time, ask for opinions or advice on your images. In return, offer the same to them. Connecting with an audience is about building a two-way relationship. It can't be sustained by only asking about what they can do for you. The more you reciprocate in the relationship, the more productive collaborations can happen.

Social media has opened the floodgates for audience collaboration. In some cases, your viewers can become partners in your photography projects. Consider them as collaborators who can accomplish projects in a way a single person can't. In December 2020, photographer Drew Nikonowicz solicited his audience with the following message: "I'm working on a video piece and I need your help! If you agree to destroy one of my prints (and document the process), I will send you two for free. One to keep and one to destroy."[32] The success of this project is based on the willingness of his audience to participate. And, in doing so, they will feel more connected to Drew's life and creative process.

By cultivating a relationship with your audience, you can ask for financial support for future projects. Resources like GoFundMe and Kickstarter are platforms where photographers can raise money to fund their creative projects. Crowdfunding helps provide money needed to produce innovative ventures. It facilitates a collaborative, financial relationship between followers and artists. The audience's ability to contribute their voice and have a greater impact has brought crowdsourcing and crowdfunding forward as legitimate and viable methods for artistic development, production, and collaboration. Photographers and audiences who can successfully negotiate this connection are most likely to develop a mutually beneficial, rewarding partnership based on reciprocity.

As an example of this crowdfunding partnership/collaboration, photographers Nicholas Kahn and Richard Selesnick (Kahn & Selesnick) launched a Kickstarter campaign to publish a series of their photographs in the form of a tarot card deck called "Carnival at the End of World." What made this project possible was the avid support of Kahn and Selesnick's audience. Through crowdsourcing, their audience contributed all the money needed to print the cards. In return, each contributor received a deck of beautifully crafted images. Everyone wins in this kind of venture!

In addition to financial support, photographers can solicit followers for resources such as suggestions for locations to photograph, things to photograph, or by providing people to photograph. You can exchange prints, trade exhibitions, or buy, sell, and trade images. When audience connections become more developed, a community of photography enthusiasts can form.

Some photographers say they don't need an audience, because they only make photos for themselves. They declare they don't need audience feedback, because the images they make look exactly the way they were envisioned. You may be one of these image-makers who isn't concerned with connecting with an audience. An example of such a person would be Vivian Maier, a prolific street photographer who remained largely unknown. During her life, the audience for her photography was only a handful of people, when Maier died, she left "150,000 negatives, more than 3,000 prints, hundreds of rolls of film."[33] It's ironic that the photos she left behind ended up attracting a worldwide audience after her death.

It's impossible to make photographs to which everyone will respond positively. Some people will like your photos and some won't. That's just the way it is, and that's OK. It makes the audience you gain more important, because they are a community of people that truly appreciate your work.

Even if you embrace the idea of an audience, never make photos to please your viewers – and that includes your instructors and classmates. Set clear boundaries between yourself and your audience. Never feel like you have to follow their dictates for your creative direction. To do so will likely lead to a dissatisfied audience and you feeling uninterested in your photography. Followers can provide feedback, but you must decide which input supports your creative vision and which doesn't. Your audience's reactions and opinions are *not* reasons to pursue your photography practice. On the other hand, reasons *to* pursue your photography practice are:

- To fulfill your creative vision.
- Because you find it meaningful.
- To find answers to questions.
- Because you are curious.

- Because you want to explore, to play, and investigate.
- To find something you are looking for.

It's important to point out that most photographs you make will only be seen by you, and that's the way it should be. When you look at the photos of an expert like Malian photographer Malick Sidibé, you are looking at a small fraction of the portraits he chose to show his viewers. Photos with closed eyes, crooked clothing, unflattering expressions, or those with a poor exposure, were surely edited out and hidden from his audience. Street photographers like Joel Meyerowitz make thousands of photos that are never seen by fans. His discriminating eye chooses exactly what he wants his audience to see. Any digital image that doesn't meet Meyerowitz's personal expectations is put in a folder that may never be opened again. Most of the photographs anyone makes will likely end up in a digital junk heap on a forgotten hard drive.

The point is that photographers put a lot of creative energy, time, and expense into making photographs, most of which don't represent the quality the creator expects. Yet, those hidden photos are critically important to the process of image-making. They represent the stages of failure and experimentation needed to arrive at a creative breakthrough. Those *in-between* photos are part of the step-by-step development process that leads you from one successful image to the next. The *in-between* photos don't need an audience.

It could be said that the most important audience for your work is the future you. You can learn a lot from looking at your old photographs, especially the ones you thought were your very best. Your photographs have a lot to teach you, and the lessons you learn can have a profound effect on your photography practice and your creative life. For this reason, and others discussed above, ultimately the most important audience for your photography is you.

9

Meet Your Community

Making photographs tends to be a solitary artform to practice. Images are conceived and generated from a private, individual perspective. Unless you work in a creative partnership, like Robert and Shana ParkeHarrison or Kahn & Selesnick, you produce photos that are solely the product of your personal creative process. It's totally up to you how you make photos that express your sense of individualism and your unique life experience. As photographers, we may tend to work alone, but as human beings we are driven to be social. Renowned psychologist Abraham Maslow believed that

> Human beings are wired to be part of a group. We evolved as an integral part of the "human tribe" … We have formed communities not just so we can feel part of something but also for survival … Our hormonal profile … dictates the biological need for belonging … Belonging is the third highest human need in Maslow's hierarchy of survival.[34]

Photographers also want to feel a sense of belonging and connection. There are many benefits that can come through being part of a group. Everyone profits from joining with like-minded people who can offer opportunities for feedback, exhibition possibilities, and to support your creative goals. Curator Rebecca Senf points out that "So much of what happens in the art world happens through connections, networks, and relationships."[35] As an emerging photographer, it's

10.4324/9781003106685-9

time to reach out and initiate those connections. Start building the foundation of your photo community.

A community is a group of people that are connected in some way. Riché C. Zamor says that, "Just as denoted by the root and the suffix of the word (common-unity), a certain segment of the population is united by a familiar thread."[36] In this case, the thread is your shared interest in photography, among all the students in your photo classes, photo program, and even those who have graduated from the program. You are also connected with many students and instructors through your common experiences at the institution where you are studying photography.

You share a common goal with lots of community members who are interested in leveling up in their photography knowledge and skills. Like you, they probably enjoy showing their work to other people. They would probably like to learn from experienced image-makers and they value feedback that can help them become more masterful photographers. Whether you are a beginner or advanced practitioner, it's important to be part of a photo community, to gain those connections that can help you achieve creative goals, academic goals, and career goals.

Research shows that you will greatly increase your odds of academic success by finding and identifying with a group of high-achieving people. Another top predictor of student success in college has to do with feeling like you are part of a community. It's within communities that you can find support networks, a sense of camaraderie, collaboration, and positive social experiences with people like you. For instance, take a look around at your photography peers. They are your immediate photographic community. In lots of ways you are all different from each other. Yet, in at least two ways you are very much alike. You all chose to attend the same class, and all of you are interested in learning photography.

These shared interests unite you in a first-level community that branches out into the world. The branches include professional photographers, press photographers, fine art photographers, and anyone else that consider themselves a maker of images. The branches form a tree, to which you belong, that reaches out to include a vast community of people. Branches include:

Level 1: Students in your photo classes and your instructors.
Level 2: Students in other sections of your photo classes and their instructors.
Level 3: Students in your photo program and their instructors.
Level 4: Former students of your program.
Level 5: Students in other academic programs and instructors (around the world).
Level 6: Photographers outside academia (local).
Level 7: Photographers outside academia (in your country).
Level 8: Photographers outside academia (around the world).

It's easy to meet new people and start friendships in your first-level community, because you are together in classes. Photographer Amanda Kohr recommends that you: find your tribe by doing some self-reflection to figure out specifically what kind of community you are looking for; are willing to try new things; attend meet-ups to get some real face-time; ditch judgment, because it negatively affects your ability to connect with others; promote and participate in your tribe; and are the first one to reach out and meet someone who is a "friendly looking stranger." If you are interested in photography, no matter what your skill level, there are people out there like you.[37]

Person-to-person connections are crucial, because every photo student could use some support when they're struggling with some part of their photo practice. For instance, in the beginning lots of students struggle to figure out the relationship between the f-number, the size of the aperture, and how that translates to depth of field. Everyone in the photo community has wrestled with finding their photographic voice. Advanced students may have put a lot of effort into intellectual demands of critical theory. Everyone is trying to gain the knowledge needed to find a path that is most personally meaningful. These are a few of the challenges we all share. Psychologist, Dr. Karyn Hall explains that "A sense of belonging to a greater community improves your motivation, health, and happiness. When you see your connection to others, you know that all people struggle and have difficult times. You are not alone."[38]

Just know that, for every struggle, every challenge, there are resources that can help within your community. For instance, even membership-driven organizations can provide supportive member benefits. A community is the perfect place to find mentors, professional references, advisors, and role models. As you transition out of your formal education, your community may have resources that can offer personal and professional support with advice and job leads.

In *The Photography Teacher's Handbook*, I said:

> Eventually students may transition from being in a learning community to a professional community composed of members that once themselves belonged to student communities. This is where professional connections are made through a network of like-minded people. If a student decides to continue to follow their interest in photography after their formal education, these communities can be critical for offering opportunities to continue to grow in photographic abilities, both technical and intellectual. Membership could also lead to future employment or critical professional advice. Participating in a photographic community can also support a photographer's aspirations for life-long learning, intellectual collaboration, and a deepening appreciation for the field.[39]

If you Google "photography community," you would get nearly six billion hits, most of which are online communities. Sites like Photo.net, Flickr, and Light Stalking are popular group sites where you can post work, promote yourself, participate in forums, and get feedback on your work. All of these communities have a place in the photo world, but no community will ever be as beneficial as one that provides opportunities for you to meet members face to face. Here are a few prospects, where you can find communities and networks:

- Take a class at a community college (even after you graduate).
- Enroll in an online course.
- Sign up for a workshop.
- Join a photo club (or start one).
- Attend a photo festival (photokina, Imaging USA, ShutterFest, Filter Photo, PhotoPlus, etc.).
- Go to photo exhibition receptions.
- Become a member of a photo organization, like the Society for Photographic Education (SPE) or WPPI, ASMP, APHE, etc. Go to photo conferences (SPE, WPPI, ASMP, APHE, etc.) The SPE community of photographers sponsors many "chapter" events throughout the year where you can show your work, receive and give critical feedback, all while networking with students, educators, professionals, and renowned photographers.

Liz Allen, SPE's Chair, says that

> The Society for Photographic Education has evolved since its founding by a handful of photography educators in Rochester, NY. Its current tag-line "understanding how photography matters in the world" is true, I believe, to its founding members' intentions. SPE was started by and has always included people involved in the academic exploration of photography as a fine art medium. Established with the Invitational Teaching Conference, SPE has grown in the last 57 years to include many more individuals, organizations and institutions. It is still first and foremost a largely volunteer, member-based community of people supporting and challenging each other as our contributions to the practice of photography and its role as a global language continues to expand our understanding of humanity. I have benefited greatly by my involvement with SPE, since I first volunteered as a grad student in 1992 at Rochester Institute of Technology.[40]

Many photo instructors are willing to help you out, no matter what your level of photographic accomplishment. They may share resources with you that support your technical, artistic, creative, and intellectual growth. Don't hesitate to ask for help or advice. You can also return the favor by helping others who aren't as far along the photography path as you.

You may also find an occasion to join smaller, specialized groups within the larger community. For example, within SPE there are groups, such as the Multicultural Caucus, the Women's Caucus, the LGBTQ Caucus, Contingent

Faculty, and the High School Educators Caucus. You could join a photo club or group interested in community volunteer projects, promoting social justice and racial equality (to name a few).

Photographer JR leads a group of image-makers who bring people together from all over the world to form a community that advocates for disadvantaged populations. JR promotes this idea by using his photos to highlight the fact that we are all part of the human community. For example, JR created a series of photos he calls Face 2 Face. He made several individual close-up portraits of Israelis and Palestinians, in which each person is making a funny face. The final images were printed in large scale and posted on both sides of the West Bank separation wall. He wants to show viewers (Israelis and Palestinians) that, even though the two communities are in conflict, they share many more similarities than differences.

JR's work reminds us that each of us can play a role as part of a worldwide community. As a member of that community, using photography as your superpower, you can change our communities for the better.

Change happens when members of a community transform themselves from being inactive members to active members. You could become involved in your classroom community if you take on a leadership role by showing up on time, being prepared to learn, participating in class activities, and helping out whenever you can. In other words, if you want to get the most out of your community experience, you'll need to become an active member of your photography program. You can also extend the range of your impact if you play a role in the larger photo community outside your institution. One way to do this is to volunteer for an organization, like SPE. Your service can have a big impact on your community and you.

1. *Psychological benefits*: Volunteering increases overall life satisfaction and helps you feel good about yourself, because you are helping others. It can also help to decrease stress and ease depression.
2. *Social benefits*: Volunteering engages students with the community, creates special bonds with the population being served, and increases social awareness and a sense of responsibility.
3. *Cognitive benefits*: "Volunteering helps students enhance their personal knowledge, grow from new experiences, and develop better interpersonal communication skills."[41]

Find out how you can support your community by taking note of what is on the leadership's list of needs. Maybe you can volunteer to work at events, send out emails, stuff swag bags, or, if you don't have any time, you could donate money or materials that would help them out. At some point you might even like to serve as part of the community's leadership. Functioning communities need members that are willing to pitch in. Plus, it's valuable experience and an impressive line item on your resume!

Your photo community is SHARED. among its members, and that is what makes it so powerful. Philosopher Jean Vanier said that

> One of the marvelous things about community is that it enables us to welcome and help people in a way we couldn't as individuals. When we pool our strength and share the work and responsibility, we can welcome many people, even those in deep distress, and perhaps help them find self-confidence and inner healing.[42]

Here is a review of what the SHARED photo community can offer:

See that community brings a sense of belonging that can increase your chances for academic success.
Helpful members provide mentors, professional references, advisors, and role models.
Active participation offers psychological, social, and cognitive benefits.
Realize that you are part of local, regional, national, and worldwide photo communities.
Empathy leads to connecting with the diversity of photographers from around the world.
Develop support networks for your creative, educational, and professional practices.

Part 3
Practice

10

Active Seeing

> Develop your own sense of seeing. Look at things. A casual glance isn't enough. Get in the habit of scanning a scene, appreciating its qualities. For, unless you get an honest bounce out of the beauties, the ironies, the design of the visible world, you can't expect your camera to give you anything but lack-luster pictures. If you delight in seeing, there's a grand chance that you'll make really fine pictures. Then, backing up your ability to really see with a sound appreciation of the technique of photography, you will make the fine pictures which, today, may seem beyond your reach.
>
> (Thomas H. Miller and Wyatt Brummitt, *This Is Photography*, 1945)[43]

A good way to understand the deliberate act of *seeing* is to compare it to the way you read. To read, you have to look at words in the sentence to derive meaning from the writing. There are different ways of reading, like skimming, reciting, and studying. When you skim, you get a superficial idea about what is being said in the text. You get a shallow, general understanding because you spend little time examining the content of the paragraphs. Skimming is a lot like how we all habitually see the world around us, with a quick glance and a limited understanding of what we perceive. If you want to grow as a photographer, it's better to practice a method of seeing that is more like *studying* what is in front of your eyes. If you improve your ability to look more thoroughly, you'll gain a sense of visual awareness that will directly impact how you perceive the world.

DOI: 10.4324/9781003106685-10

With that awareness you'll notice things that you had not seen before. Some of those things may inspire you to photograph them. And that inspiration could appear as part of the image!

Rather than look in a passive way at the world, find visual relationships, and look with depth. If you just scan a scene with your camera, you might quickly judge whether or not it's worth photographing. When you observe with depth, you can experience the subject in a way that goes beyond the reflex response of whether you like it or don't like it. If you get past your superficial reaction, the scene can reveal itself to be something visually and/or conceptually interesting and worth photographing. Consciously knowing there is a way of responding beyond those two choices (like and don't like) can compel you to capture meaningful images, interesting, thought-provoking, or noteworthy in so many ways. It can teach you to question your first impression about the photographic potential of a subject during a first glance, then to continue looking.

Your ability to intentionally observe a scene is important for two reasons. First, it will provide direct experiences that contribute to your becoming more visually aware as a photographer. As your eyes gather information, whatever you see could become material for your creative process. Seeing and storing the visual impressions of things, like what is happening around you, will increase your chances of inventing and capturing unique images. Second, seeing is important, because when you look at photographs you need to be able to perceive and understand all of the visual elements in a composition, to derive meaning from what you see, and to develop visual fluency so you are able to offer insights about what you observe.

You can counteract the habit of skimming by learning and practicing how to slow down enough that you can observe what is really in front of your eyes. Amy E. Herman said:

> Ironically, it is often the simple, the everyday, and the familiar that we have trouble describing because we have ceased to notice what makes them interesting and unusual. By adulthood, we become so inured to the complexity of the world that only the new, the innovative, and the exigent capture our attention and dominate our field of vision. We rely on experience and intuition rather than seeking out nuances and details that can make a difference in our success. Yet, it is the things that we see and negotiate on a regular basis to which we must be especially attuned.[44]

The kind of seeing that Herman is talking about is the practice of learning how to manage your own attention span.

Seeing with intention is the key to unlocking the secrets of Leonardo da Vinci's personal practice of Saper Vedere (meaning "knowing how to see"). One way to start improving is by studying the work of old master painters. Historical artists like da Vinci, Johannes Vermeer, Rembrandt van Rijn, and others used their powers of observation to gain a lot of awareness into the way light, shadow, and color communicate in a scene. Another reason why these artists' paintings are so beneficial to study is because they were skillful and deliberate in the way they observed all aspects of a scene and could reproduce what they perceived onto canvas.

Begin developing your powers of observation by noting how far (physical distance) your eyes are from the canvas or the photograph. You need to be close enough to see details, yet far enough away to see the whole scene. When observing an artwork, there is a formula for how far your face should be from the piece. For a two-dimensional artwork, your eyes need to be at a distance equal to the measurement between its two opposing corners. For example, if you are looking at an 8 × 10 inch (203 × 254 mm) print, your eyes should be roughly 12.5 inches (300 mm) from the surface of the image. In other words, to actively examine a photo or painting, you have to be close enough or far enough away to see the overall composition and the details.

The correct viewing distance allows you to accurately perceive enough visual evidence to answer the questions "What am I looking at? What is this image about? What is it in this composition that compelled the photographer to purposefully capture this photo?" Or, "What story is this painter describing for me? What do they want me to see, feel, and understand?" Collect information by allowing your attention to look at all the elements in the image. This is the only way to become fully conscious of it, to discover everything it's offering. You may have to physically stand up and move closer to arrive at the realizations that can only come from fully identifying what's in front of you. Be aware that, whatever information you don't consciously notice with your eyes, your brain will fill in those gaps with assumptions, made from mining your memories.

Seeing *deliberately* helps you maximize the processing power of your brain by steering away from other sensory distractions, including thinking. When looking, stay focused. Your purpose is to actively look, not think about what you see. It's helpful to be curious about what you're looking at, but you will be more observant if you aren't talking, listening to music, checking texts, or following distractions. It's also helpful if you slow down your viewing speed so you can focus. First-time practitioners might need a little more time and that's OK. Stow your phone someplace for 10 minutes. The more you practice looking, the more you'll start noticing lots of things in other parts of your life, like details in movies, connections between homework assignments for other classes, and important visual details in the environment around you.

Soon you will be asked to look at a painting online. You could use your phone, but a computer would be better, because the larger screen will allow you to see more overall detail. Before you go online, embrace your inner Sherlock Holmes, the superhero of curiosity, observation, and deduction. His superpower is the ability to notice subtle clues and aspects of a scene that others commonly overlook. As Mr. Holmes once said, "The world is full of obvious things which nobody by any chance ever observes." Holmes points out that he sees "no more than you, but I have trained myself to notice what I see." The exercise you are about to do helps you practice Holmes' ability so that, as you develop your skills, you can take advantage of the photographic rewards![45]

In this exercise, Make an Inventory, you list what you see, and it works best if you do it with a partner. Begin individually, without collaborating or talking about what you each discover. Your goal is to practice seeing and observing as you each compile a list of everything you observe. The inventory should be objective, including only what you perceive. In other words, you are simply noting what you recognize, solely based on evidence and not on assumptions, prior information, or opinions. For example, there is either a person in the image or there isn't. Try to find and identify everything you can.

Note every visual element you see. Start with the most prominent visual subjects in the frame, then work your way down to the small details. Look for sections where the painter placed the most visual emphasis. If you see something you can't identify, just note that you don't know what it is, but describe its visual qualities, like its shape or color.

After you make an inventory, it's helpful to describe locations where elements are, generally within the frame of the composition. Include observations on how many of the same things there are, people, and objects, and notable special relationships between subjects (whether they are far apart, close together, or overlapping).

Look closely at lighting characteristics, shadows, and colors. Note the quality of light (hard or soft), direction of light, intensity of light, and overall color cast from the light. Shadows are also important. Shadows give you clues about the quality and direction of light, along with information on the number of light sources.

To get you in the right mindset, imagine that you have to describe the artwork to someone who can't see it. The only way they can visualize the composition in front of you is based on the accuracy of your description. Be specific in the way you communicate the image's contents. I suspect that Holmes' advice would be: "stick to the facts."

Now it's time to practice by looking at a visually complex painting. Team up with a partner. You will begin without any information, such as the artist's name and title of the work, because it could influence your observations. The big question to answer is, "What do you see?" If you must use your phone to examine the painting, and the image is too small to see the details, then zoom in. Make a thorough list, but don't expect to note every single element. To make sure the inventories don't get too long, give yourself a time limit, perhaps 10 minutes.

When you and your partner are finished, you can compare notes on what you observed. Find out the things you missed and those your partner missed. Of course, whoever finds the most wins! If you both are able to see most of what is in the painting, you both win! If you missed a lot of things, it just means you need some practice. Few people will be able to see everything, especially in 10 minutes.

Set a timer on your phone and get on your computer. For a live link to the painting, go to www.photostudent.net and look under the "Resources" heading for "Seeing Practice." When you arrive, begin your visual inventory. Don't turn this page until you have finished.

Here is the site:

www.metmuseum.org/art/collection/search/626692

Now flip this page to reveal the results of the exercise.

Compare what you saw with what your partner noticed, then list the differences. Did you both notice the things below?

- A sculpture of a lion attacking the elk in the upper right corner.
- There are two dogs.
- A woman is sitting on a platform.
- The man and the girl in the center have ribbons on their shoes.
- The main light for the scene is hard and is somewhere high and to the right side of the subjects.
- A man is pointing to a bible.
- The floor is made of marble.
- The lady is wearing pearls.
- The girl on the right is the only person looking at the viewer.

When you practice any kind of mental or physical ability, that ability gets stronger. When you deliberately try to throw a ball through a hoop, over and over, the repetition and refinement of your practice changes the physiological structure of your brain. Your brain responds the same way when you deliberately practice seeing and observing. It reconfigures networks to become more observant. Practice transforms your old habit of seeing into a new, more skillful, way of seeing. The reason why we do this is because, as Alexander Graham Bell once said, "We are all too much inclined to walk through life with our eyes shut. There are things all around us and right at our very feet that we have never seen because we have never really looked."[46]

Another seeing exercise you can do with your partner is called Describe and Draw. For this, one of you starts by choosing a photographic image, while keeping it hidden from the other person. You could also use a painting. For the sake of time, I suggest you use a composition that isn't too visually complex. The other person has a pencil and a drawing pad or piece of paper. The person with the image verbally describes the image, while the other attempts to draw solely from the description.

This practice requires the "describing" person to look closely, to be very specific in their description of shapes, forms, textures, and where the elements are located in the frame. In other words, before they can tell someone else what to draw, the viewer has to deliberately observe the whole of the artwork and make an inventory.

Think of the rectangle of the page or frame as a grid, like the rule of thirds. This will help you describe the location of objects and forms in terms of grid coordinates. The "drawing" person is free to ask questions, in order to clarify any details they don't understand. If you are the "describing" person, begin by establishing the format of the artwork – whether it is square, or a landscape vs. portrait format. From there, be descriptive.

Doing these exercises is like going through "seeing boot camp" in preparation for observing images as part of your photo practice. These exercises are also important for becoming an image-maker/observer of the world. The valuable skills you acquire with these practices come into play when you are actively photographing and when looking at photos in critique. It doesn't matter whether you are walking around looking for something to photograph or building a tableau, as a large part of your creative practice is observation. Your ability to see with awareness and clarity will directly relate to the visual and conceptual qualities of your photos.

As you practice, you will gain insights and start to recognize those things that either support or detract from your creative, visual story. Professional dancer and author on creativity Twyla Tharp teaches that "Everything is raw material. Everything is relevant. Everything is usable. Everything feeds into my creativity. But without proper preparation, I cannot see it, retain it, and use it."[47] Ultimately, photography helps you become more observant, so you can see the world more clearly, even during those times when you aren't holding a camera.

11

Develop Your Perception of Light

With every photo you compose, consider light to be one of the main subjects. Observe how light either enhances or detracts from the impact of everything in the frame. Light makes the image possible while it also shapes the viewer's understanding of the scene. It controls the sense of drama, concept, perception of textures, the illusion of form, and the way colors are depicted. Your skillful use of light can potentially elevate the most boring, banal subject matter, making it appear remarkable. As Aaron Rose once said, "In the right light, at the right time, everything is extraordinary."[48]

Every serious photographer is a student of light. If you want to become a masterful image-maker, study light as part of your path. Also, become photographically literate, practice your visual skills enough to become fluent in the technical, conceptual, and visual aspects of the medium. To be fluent in the photographic art, you must be able to understand and thoughtfully utilize the language of light as the thread that runs through all photographic concerns.

Study how light behaves. Experiment with how you can use it to communicate the story you want your images to tell, for "Lighting is the language of photography. Patterns of light convey information just as surely as spoken words … Lighting, like any other language, has a grammar and a vocabulary."[49] Your capacity to consciously perceive, understand, and make use of light is directly related to your level of photographic learning and experience. The skillful use of light contributes to and supports a narrative.

Turn your awareness toward the interplay of light and shadow, and learn about the visual cues the human brain seeks to perceive form, texture, and

10.4324/9781003106685-11

dimension. Imagine yourself as a crime scene investigator (CSI) and fix your attention on the spectacle in front of you. Analyze the evidence that provides visual cues that point to what the light is communicating. You may notice how the direction of light enhances the appearance of texture and form. The direction and quality of hard light can also make colors appear vibrant. Soft light can make the colors look muted. One of your objectives is to observe and understand how light describes a story.

The behavior of light is largely predictable, yet its characteristics are affected by many factors. Professor of Neuroscience and author Beau Lotto, in his book *Deviate*, points out that

> we think of daylight as a simple journey from the sun to our eyes, the quality of the light that eventually hits our eyes is determined by three different sources. Of course, the first is the sun itself. The second is reflectors, the billions of surfaces that surround us at any moment in time. And finally, the source as transmitters – the space between you and the objects, like the air.[50]

In your photos, especially your color images, think about how these three factors influence your perception of a scene. Observe how light shapes the visual characteristics of the elements in your images.

Do you ever wonder where our photographic concepts around light and lighting come from? David Hockney once said that 16th-century Italian painter Caravaggio "invented Hollywood lighting."[51] Caravaggio, along with Flemish painter Peter Paul Rubens, and 17th-century Dutch painters Rembrandt and Vermeer, clearly had an intimate understanding of how light behaves and the way it could communicate emotion, mood, and atmosphere in their masterpieces.

These painters' profound knowledge regarding the characteristics of light – like *quality*, *direction*, *intensity*, *color*, and *light-to-shadow ratios* – enabled each of them to translate the attributes of light onto canvas in a way that expressed their individual interpretations of their subjects. By doing so, they enhanced the work's visual impact through the illusion of realism. They skillfully conveyed light and shadow through the application of paint on flat, two-dimensional surfaces. Their expert handling of paint leaves viewers no choice but to perceive the illuminated subjects as three-dimensional.

In many ways these painters' treatment of light serves to teach you, a 21st-century photographer, how to understand and identify the characteristics of light. The good news is that you can learn the same way they did it – by intentionally observing and using the active seeing methods covered in the previous chapter. You can come to understand why their centuries-old observations are still important today! Looking at the works of the above painters can help you develop a sense of awareness around how light performs. When you are able to see the light, you can apply what you learn to your image-making practice, the photos you critique, and the scenes you photograph.

The key to learning is to know exactly what you are looking for. Get online and find a photograph from Joel Sartore's series "The Photo Ark." When you find an image, look for visual evidence that will help identify the *quality of light* (hard or soft). Look at the shadows and where the shadows meet the planes of light. Highlighting areas and shadows will tell you whether the light is hard, soft, or somewhere in between. If the shadows are distinct, dark, and defined, then this indicates the light is hard. If there is an emphasis on form and texture, then the light is hard. In the scene, there may be little evidence of texture or surface details due to a lack of shadows. If the scene also appears flat and the colors seem subdued, then this evidence points to the presence of soft lighting.

The next characteristic is the *direction of light*, which refers to where the brightest light source is positioned in relationship to the scene. In addition, direction must also take into consideration where the camera is located. For example, let's say you are photographing a friend who is illuminated by the setting sun, coming from the horizon at the right of the subject's position. That direction of light will change if the photographer moves and puts the subject between the sun and the camera. Now the direction of light is from behind the subject. As you can see, the direction of light can only be understood by considering all three of these elements and the positional relationships they share:

1. Components in the scene.
2. The camera.
3. The main light source.

In order to figure out the direction of light, note the direction in which the shadows are falling away from the subject. Light travels in straight lines, so if you visualize an imaginary line, from a point on the edge of a shadow to its corresponding point on an outline of the subject, that line will lead directly to the light source. You can also find where the specular highlights appear on shiny surfaces (like the eyes) to provide evidence. It's easy to find the direction of light with hard lighting, because there are distinct highlights and shadows. Soft light, on the other hand, doesn't produce as many well-defined clues.

Think about the low-contrast lighting on a cloudy day. Sunlight is modified by clouds, which cause the light rays to scatter in many directions. To figure out where the sun is in this case, you must identify the areas of greater light intensity. You don't have shadows, but you can look for any kind of diffused highlights to figure out the trajectory that points back to the area of clouds that is brightest.

The direction of light is essential in photography, because it connects to deep psychological and emotional aspects of human perception. We relate the position of light sources to our experience of the sun. It feels natural when light comes from somewhere between horizon level and directly above. Sunlight doesn't naturally come from below us. When we see a face lit from below, we react with discomfort and fear. That natural sense of unease created by using a low position makes it a perfect direction for horror movies!

In a studio, you are free to change the direction of light by moving the main light wherever you want. When you're photographing outside, you can't move the sun to a favorable position. Sometimes, however, you can move your subject to change its relationship to the light source. If you can't move your subject, you can change your vantage point in relation to the subject, thus changing the perceived position of the sun. If the sun is at your back, the subject will receive frontal lighting. If the subject is between you and the light source, the subject will be backlit.

The direction of light is immediately and unconsciously interpreted by viewers. They unknowingly react with psychological and emotional responses. For example, hard lighting from the side can create a sense of drama in a photo. Frontal, soft lighting visually flattens the subject by removing the appearance of form and texture to convey feelings of calmness or stillness. Specific lighting positions can make human subjects look friendly, strong, authoritative, beautiful, or dangerous and menacing.

The next characteristic of light is *intensity*, which can be understood as the level of brightness in a scene. Intensity is a characteristic that's difficult to assess when looking at photos, because the photographer can use their exposure settings to compensate for the light intensity in the scene. The Arizona desert sun will have a high intensity, yet can appear normal in a photo, because the photographer can adjust the camera's ISO, aperture, and shutter speed to reduce the amount of light that will fall on the CCD and thus normalize the appearance of the scene in the photo. As a result, the visual evidence in the image may not reflect the actual intensity of the light when the photo was made.

Intensity of light really comes into play when making photos, because it will greatly influence the camera settings available to you during your production phase. The greater the intensity of the light in your scene, the more creative freedom you will have to choose the quality of your photo (ISO), how much depth of field you want to include (aperture), and whether or not you want to freeze motion with faster shutter speeds. Low-intensity lighting, on the other hand, limits you to high ISO settings, shallow depth of field, and slower shutter speeds.

When you're photographing someone outside in sunlight, you can lower the intensity of the light on your subject by moving them to and from shaded areas of the scene. You can also use modifiers, like a diffusion panel placed between the sun and the subject. If you are using an artificial light source in the studio, you can move it closer to the subject to increase intensity, and farther away to lower the intensity. Some lights even allow you to adjust the power output of the illumination.

When *color* is talked about as a characteristic of light, it refers to a light source's *color temperature*. Color temperature refers to a scientific method used to identify the prominent color in a light source, which can range from warm, or red (1,000° Kelvin), to cool, or blue (10,000° Kelvin). Most people don't notice the dominant color of a light source, but it's there. This is because your brain uses its color filtration system to remove the dominant color cast from your perception, so everything in the scene appears to be properly color balanced. For example, daylight tends to be bluish, at around 5500° Kelvin. You don't notice a blue cast on everything when you are outdoors, because your brain compensates by removing some of the blue hue from your perception.

Digital cameras don't work as well as your brain when color-correcting light temperatures, but they do a pretty good job balancing the colors in your photos. If your camera makes a mistake, you can easily adjust the color temperature in post-production when using RAW files. Be aware that your camera can only balance the color of a single light source. You may see color shifts in a photo when there is more than one kind of light in a scene, like tungsten, sodium vapor, or LED. Color temperature is most important to understand when making photos, but it also comes into play when viewing images.

If you look at a photo that includes a scene with lights that are orange, pink, blue, or yellow, you'll understand that it's likely due to the camera's inability to render multiple color temperatures at the same time. Your eyes are the same, in that they can't balance a mixed-light situation. Try to see if you can identify different colors of light in such a scene. For some examples of mixed lighting, take a look at *National Geographic* photographer Jim Richardson's night photography.

The last characteristic of light to know is *lighting ratios*. Lighting ratios directly relate to contrast. The greater the difference between the bright areas of your scene and the darkest shadows, the greater the lighting ratio and the "higher" contrast you will have. It's the difference between the intensity of main light and the amount of light in the shadows. If you have a main light and a second light with the same intensities, the lighting ratio would be 1:1. As you lower the intensity of the second (fill) light, the difference in light to darkness changes. You start to get shadows from the main light as the intensity of the fill light goes down. The darker the shadows get, the left number in the ratio (the main light) goes up. A high-contrast image could have a ratio of 128:1. If you are interested in learning more, Google "lighting ratios" to learn the formulas for calculating the ratios.

Now that you have a basic understanding of the characteristics of light, let's explore how to put that knowledge to use. Imagine, again, that you are a CSI. You walk into a room and immediately focus on the details in the scene, so you can understand the story this place has to tell. The room holds forensic information about a mysterious event. You can figure out what happened if you are perceptive enough to see the evidence that is hidden in plain sight. If you want to learn what light has to teach, you must approach the lighting in a scene in this way.

Start by exercising your perception of light. Whether you're looking at an actual location or a scene in a photograph, begin by identifying both the quality of light and the direction of light from the main light source. You learned above where to look for evidence. Next, on a scale of 0 to 10, with 10 being high contrast and 0 being very low contrast, assign a number for the contrast (ratio of light to dark). Then, answer these two questions:

1. How is the quality of light affecting the appearance of the scene?
2. What is that effect communicating to you, the viewer?

Go further. What part does that quality of light play in the mood or drama in the scene? Do you think the quality of light contributes to the message that the other elements in the scene are communicating? Let your curiosity guide you. Next, follow the same steps with the direction of light.

Try to apply what you have learned. Get online and search for Edward Weston's black-and-white photo *Pepper No. 30*. Look for the light. What do you see?

Try again with Alessandra Sanguinetti's photo *The Necklace*. Look closely for evidence. What kind of light source do you think is being used to illuminate the photo?

Now search *Mars and Rhea Silvia*, by Peter Paul Rubens. Look at the way light is used on the main figures, and also identify any discrepancies in the lighting.

Take a look at Freddy Fabris' photo *The Last Supper*. What do your eyes tell you about the lighting in this photo?

Lastly, analyze the light in Caravaggio's painting *Supper at Emmaus*.[52] If you can, print out a photocopy so there is a large white border around the artwork. Draw lines from subjects and objects in the painting to the light sources that are outside the scene. This will help you find the direction of light. What is the quality of light, and why do you think Caravaggio chose this approach? How do light intensity and color temperature play a role in the scene? The lighting seems obvious at first glance. A closer look reveals that Caravaggio took some artistic liberties with how he lit these individual characters. There is an unsolved mystery with the light reflected from the table and onto the face of the man in the lower left of the composition.

Once you are able to observe how the light behaves in the above photos, establish a habit of doing this practice with other photos you see. It's also beneficial to do it when watching movies. They are great for examining light! As a final practice, enhance your perception and understanding of light by analyzing scenes in real life. Wherever you are – walking across campus, in a classroom, eating lunch, or doing your homework – take note of how the light is behaving and how that communicates something about the scene. Pause for a moment where you are right now, and identify the quality and direction of the light. Learn to see when light is supporting your ideas and when it's working against your goals. Once you are able to recognize how the light is behaving, you can use your skills to manipulate it so the light enhances the visual and conceptual impact of your own images.

12

Critique and the Seven Cs

There is no better way to grow in your photography practice than by giving and receiving useful feedback through critiques. The process can give rise to novel insights that will help you and others become more skillful, perceptive photographers. The practice helps everyone develop a capacity for analytical and critical thinking. It also cultivates important observational skills that can be used in all dimensions of image-making. As you become more perceptive, you'll be able to reveal and understand meaningful aspects in both your own and other's photos.

Critique is a procedure that can be broken down into four parts, where students are expected to:

1. Present photographs to be critiqued.
2. Receive feedback from others.
3. Critically examine and comment on photographic images.
4. Compose and present an artist statement about your work and practice (optional).

When critique day arrives, be prepared. Have your photos ready to present and turn in. Prepare the images in the format(s) required by your instructor. Note that the presentation format and the turn-in formats may be different. Take a little time before class to psychologically and emotionally prepare yourself for feedback during class. Grab your notebook and a pen. When all these steps are finished, you are ready to show your photos to the class!

10.4324/9781003106685-12

When you learn how others respond to your work, it can give you a better understanding of your photos. Perceptive observations can provide critical information that you may need to help you reach the next level of creative growth. When you achieve some degree of mastery over your observational skills, you may be able to gain insights into your own work. Even so, you'll come to rely on others to give thoughtful commentary.

Meaningful feedback in critiques can come in two forms, as timely feedback or general feedback. Timely feedback refers to suggestions for improvement that can be applied immediately to your images. This kind of advice includes local and global editing, like cropping, color, or contrast adjustments. It could also address ideas for how to best present your images. For example, you may learn in critique that your photos could have more visual impact if you change their presentation size. Timely feedback is valuable, because it provides suggestions that you can try immediately and see if they actually do improve the work.

The second kind of input comes as general feedback. These comments are information that you can't apply to the photos being critiqued. You can only consider these observations to enhance future photography. This might include suggestions for changing up your vantage points, moving your subject to another part of the composition, using a different quality of light, or evoking a greater variety of expressions on a model. This kind of criticism may address your fundamental habits and approach to photography, so it's something to be aware of during the planning and production phases of subsequent assignments.

In the classroom, feedback can come from both your peers or your instructors. Depending on the format of your critiques, your instructor may give remarks during the in-class critique and also as written comments during grading. If you want to get the most out of a critique, while at the same time impressing your instructor, seriously consider the advice you receive in critiques. Pay close attention to those pointed suggestions that your instructor offers. If you receive an idea that you think could improve your photos, then take the time to try it out. It's disappointing for an instructor when students receive valuable feedback on their work and those same photos end up in their final portfolio without any of the suggestions being considered or applied.

If you want to impress your instructor, come to critique prepared to take notes. When you write notes, it communicates that you believe what other people have to say is valuable. Plus, sometimes during critique it's hard to psychologically and emotionally take in all the feedback. Being in the spotlight can feel overwhelming, like sensory overload. Note-taking can help you hear more clearly by focusing your attention on what is being said in the moment. It also offers the opportunity to go back later and reconsider the comments. In any case, note-taking will assure that you won't forget someone's advice later, especially at a time when you might really need it. Note the date, the time, the work being critiqued, and the names of those giving the feedback.

Another way to get the most out of critiques is to take on a leadership role by actively participating in critique discussions. You will be expected to critique your classmates' photography. Your goal when giving a critique is to look at the images that have been presented, look closely, think, and express insightful, informed observations based on the visual and conceptual information you perceive in the work. Even if the process is hard, participate. Once you feel comfortable enough with the process, get your classmates involved.

The more you can encourage classmates to be part of a multi-student discussion, the more everyone's creative insights will emerge. University of California, Berkeley psychologist Charlan Nemeth did a study that found that criticism and debate "do not inhibit ideas but, rather, stimulate them." According to Nemeth,

> the reason criticism leads to more new ideas is that it encourages us to fully engage with the work of others. We think about their concepts because we want to improve them; it's the imperfections that lead us to really listen. (And isn't that the point of a group? If we're not here to make one another better, then why are we here?)[53]

A really good tool for increasing the depth of the critique discussion is an artist statement. The photographer can present a brief account on the background and inspirations for their work at the time the images are presented. The writing doesn't have to be a formal statement. It can be just long enough to give some kind of useful background information as the viewer looks at the photos. For example, a student may simply say, "I made these photos for an assignment on the things I am most grateful for in my life" or "This work is a response to my feelings of anxiety." The statements can be made either before or after the images are viewed. Whether or not you are required to prepare a statement is up to your instructor. The purposes of an artist statement are to:

- Assist the photographer in becoming more insightful about their own work.
- Help the photographer become more articulate when talking about their work.
- Broaden the viewer's understanding of your photo practice.
- Offer a context for the images so the reviewers can provide meaningful feedback.

The last helpful piece of advice is actually a collection of beneficial tips designed to raise your level of learning and engagement. It's an acronym called the "Seven Cs of Critique": Courage, Collaboration, Communication, C-ing, Critical thinking, Clarity, and Conclusion.

1. COURAGE

Your brain helps you in a lot of ways you don't realize. For example, right now it's keeping you alive by pumping your heart and making your lungs breathe.

Sometimes your brain reacts to situations, like a critique, with habitual fear, anxiety, or anger. When you stop and think about it, there are probably more appropriate and productive responses to giving and receiving feedback.

For instance, you might experience a fear or anxiety response when you think about putting your photos up for other people to analyze. You may feel triggered at the idea of being the sole focus of your entire class's attention. These are good examples of why it's important to be aware of how your brain habitually reacts so you can recognize it for what it is – a habit. Identifying the habit can awaken your sense of courage. If you have the strength to see what's happening, you can think it through and consider more rational ways to respond, like with curiosity, willingness, openness, or receptivity.

Here are some real-life student responses to the idea of critique:

I don't want to say anything.
I'm afraid about what other people will say about my work.
I don't want people to look at my photos, because I don't have any talent.
It makes me mad when people tell me how I can improve my work.
My work isn't nearly as good as …
This turned out exactly the way I want it to, so I don't need a critique.
I don't care what other people think of my photos.
I just want to know if my photo is good or bad.

Here are some mindful, beneficial, alternatives for responding:

What I have to say is valuable.
I am in charge and I can either accept or not accept what people say about my work.
I want to grow as a photographer and this process will help me.
If what that person says is valid, they will back it up with evidence.
Comparing my work to others' work is unproductive. Instead, I will focus on achieving my goals.
I'm happy with my work, but I'm also open to how other people see it.
Other people may have valuable feedback that can help me become a better photographer.
I'm interested in knowing what other people see in my work.

If you feel some apprehension before a critique, just know that it's completely natural to be nervous. When your work is on view, you might feel a little vulnerable and exposed, especially if it's one of your first critiques. The situation can feel unpredictable, because you don't know what people are going to say. Being courageous means recognizing those fears while participating in the critique anyway. Besides, your critique almost surely isn't going to be as traumatic as you think it will be.

Your classroom is most likely a very safe place. You will probably find there are some rules of etiquette established by your instructor to support you to feel safe and confident. Here are some commonsense rules to help you keep your attention focused on being more objective during the critique.

When you look at a photograph, your first reaction is probably, "Where does this fall on the scale between 'I love it and I hate it'?" Or, your reaction may be, "I don't care." In other words, your immediate response could be to judge the photos as either good or bad. Everyone responds in this way. The trick is to feel these reactions come up and then move on to more thoughtful responses.

For example, instead of using value judgments like "good" or "bad," think in terms of "Does this photograph meet the criteria and/or objectives for the assignment?" To be objective, you should be able to cite specific evidence in the composition to support your claim. For instance, the assignment might be focused on arranging a still-life and the instructions specifically say, "You must compose groups of inanimate objects for your photos." If there are a bunch of objects grouped into a composition, then the photo meets the criteria. If the image is a portrait, then it doesn't meet the assignment criteria. The evidence is there or it isn't. (For more discussion on what it means for a photo to be regarded as "good" or "bad," please see Chapter 33, posted online, titled Is This Photo Good or Bad?)

Instead of using the subjective words that describe your personal reaction, such as "I like" or "I don't like," think of photos in terms of whether or not the photos are working compositionally, conceptually, and/or technically. For example, maybe a photo is cropped in a way that uses all the compositional space to talk about an event happening in a scene. This aspect of the photo is "working." At the same time, the subject was composed in the dead center of the photo without featuring a sense of symmetry. This is "not working" compositionally, because it tends to draw the eye to the center and hold attention in that area. In this case, you might make a general suggestion that the photographer try to be aware of the centrally focused composition and try next time to use the rule of thirds.

Whatever happens during your critique, let your courage guide you while knowing that you can't control what other people say about your photos. You can only control your reaction to what they say, knowing that, whatever comments they make, you have the power to decide which observations are valuable and which ones aren't. This knowledge can help you be courageous throughout a critique.

2. COLLABORATION

The purpose of critique isn't to listen to a bunch of individuals telling you what you did right and what you did wrong. Instead, it's an event where everyone in the class collaborates with the purpose of achieving a single goal, to help each student improve their photo skills and abilities. Critique discussion provides an opportunity for critical self-reflection while offering the support and encouragement needed to grow as a photographer.

Think interdependently. When the whole class contributes during a critique, it builds a foundation of understanding and trust where each person becomes familiar with every other person's creative growth process. This kind of sharing builds and strengthens bonds between you and your classmates. It helps you feel connected and supports a sense of community. Positive critique experiences help unite your community, while boosting productivity. The more students understand the critique experience as a collaborative effort, the more valuable it will be as an exercise for everyone's creative growth in your photo community.

One way you can be supportive and collaborative is to be encouraging. When you see a classmate work really hard and go far beyond simply doing the minimum to complete the assignment, praise their effort. Support them on their creative efforts, be happy for them, and tell them that their hard work paid off. When you affirm others' successes, it helps everyone to want to work harder for their own success.

Critique also supports a collaborative work ethic. When a deadline is set for a critique, you can make a timeline to help you organize the stages of your assignment (pre-production through post-production) and a target date to work toward. In fact, everyone is working toward that common goal. Hopefully everyone collaborates by feeling like they are accountable to their classmates, to show up prepared with a finished assignment, ready for critique.

3. COMMUNICATION

The third of the Seven Cs of Critique is communication. Your willingness to communicate verbally is important for a successful critique. Take the opportunity to practice using the language of objective analysis, so you can improve your communication skills. For instance, critique isn't about judging the value of anyone's photos. Therefore, the words "good" or "bad" aren't used in a critique. As mentioned, comments such as "I like" or "I don't like" tend to be banned from discussion. It's a superficial response akin to clicking a "like" button on social media. These responses refer to the viewer's preferences and have nothing to do with the photos being reviewed. In his book *Depth of Field*, author A. D. Coleman says, "Nothing closes off a discussion of a work of art so completely as the assertion, 'I like it'."[54] Everyone practices using language that is objective, non-threatening, non-opinionated, impersonal, evidence-based, and, most of all, supportive and helpful. *Using* a language, any language, is how you learn to communicate effectively in that language.

Articulate your thoughts when both offering and receiving a critique. Your classmates benefit when you speak up and express your perceptions. If you hesitate because you feel like what you have to say isn't important, remember that this is a learning practice that helps you become more fluent and thoughtful with the language of critique. Try to be as insightful as you can. Do the best you can to provide observations and suggestions for improvement. Be generous when offering positive comments. Your perceptions are important.

Communication also means being able to listen. When you receive a critique, make notes and try to listen as closely as you can to what other people have to say. When your peers say something, it could create an opening for you to respond. Speak up and ask for clarification on any feedback you don't fully understand. Ask speakers to elaborate on comments that you think could lead to useful suggestions or information. The more information you actively draw out of your critique, the more possibilities you will gain for improving your photo practice.

4. C-ING

OK, "c-ing" isn't actually a word, but it's a creative way of saying "seeing," or the practice of looking. You need to be able to observe with clarity the contents of a photograph before you can offer a valuable critique. Photos may be presented as prints on a wall or they might appear digitally on a screen. Stand up and move closer if you have to. This is called *zooming in with your feet.* Your perceptions won't be relevant unless you see everything in the composition. Otherwise, your critique will be like talking about a book you haven't read.

5. CRITICAL THINKING

Critical thinking is your ability to problem-solve conceptual, technical, and compositional issues in the images you make and see. The more deliberately you observe the elements in a composition, the more likely it is that you can formulate ideas about what you think is happening. When you look at an image, how does it perform in the theater of your mind? How do the elements in the photo work together to describe the scene? How would you express your experience of looking at the photo? Each photo tells a story, or many stories. The story could be interesting, exciting, confusing, or pointless. Use the visual evidence you collect to formulate ideas and topics for discussion.

At the end of the critique, come up with at least one suggestion (timely or general) that can help the photographer improve their image-making skills. Keep in mind that there isn't a photo in existence that's perfect. Everyone can benefit from the perspectives of others. Without the chance of receiving relevant insights, there would be "no incentive to think about someone else's thoughts or embrace unfamiliar possibilities. And so the problem remains impossible. The absence of criticism has kept us all in the same place ... criticism ... acts like a multiplier for the imagination."[55]

Critical thinking is hard. When you look at a photo, give yourself time to think about what you see, but never choose to opt out of contributing. You might feel the impulse to say, "I don't know./I can't think of anything to say./ There is nothing to say." But these reactions aren't true, as there is always something that can be said. Take the opportunity to practice critical thinking and talk about what you see. Strengthen your ability to formulate and verbalize your observations.

6. CLARITY

The idea of clarity can be applied to several aspects of critique. For instance, feedback during critique should be clear. Comments are most helpful when they are understandable, specific, usable, and helpful.

Clarity, observational-analytical clarity, is also an important goal to achieve with your own work. It's very hard for anyone to see their own work with clarity, in an objective way. When you look at your own work, your perspective is biased due to all the memories, opinions, and ideas that are attached to the sensory experiences you gain when you make your images.

For example, when you see one of your own photos, you also remember being at the location, what the day was like, how you felt, the people you met, and how that photo either met your expectations or fell short of how you intended it to perform visually or conceptually. As a result, you can feel emotionally and psychologically invested in a way that prevents you from seeing your photos with new eyes, as if you were seeing them for the first time.

Sometimes this phenomenon is described as "not having enough distance" from your own photos. It's when you find it hard to be emotionally or conceptually impartial toward your work. When you don't have distance or clarity, you might interpret helpful criticism as commentary about you personally. That's why you must come to rely on others to help inform your sense of clarity for your own photos. This kind of clarity can lead to actionable ideas for improving your work. It could even spark ideas for new photos. In turn, you can try to help others achieve that same clarity for their work.

7. CONCLUSIONS

You worked hard to finish these photos and put them up in front of your classmates. Each critique represents a marker on the timeline of your journey through the levels of photographic achievement. Be proud of where you are in your photographic journey and what you've accomplished. Your successes and your mistakes have a big impact on the development of your photographic life and even on the lives of other aspiring photographers.

Consider which comments are important and which ones aren't. You may even receive feedback from two sources that conflict. One classmate may think your use of hard lighting is working really well to support the story in the photo. Another person may say that soft lighting would be more successful. You might also discover that the least valuable feedback can come from the lovers and haters of your work. Strong emotional biases can prevent reviewers from making objective, helpful comments.

At the end of the critique, you are left with a lot of information about your work. You'll find yourself in a position where you have to make an informed decision regarding how you will proceed with your photography practice. You must reach conclusions about how critiques affect your perception of your work and decide where you will go from here. It's up to you to decide which advice, if any, you will use, and which doesn't apply and can be discarded.

Find ways to apply the new information you have learned to future work. Refine your ideas, re-evaluate your purpose, and come up with new creative solutions for how to go forward. The conclusion of every critique is an exciting time, full of potential for new directions, creative development, and artistic growth.

13

Tips for Unpacking Critical Theory

Curiosity is a powerful motivating force. Philosopher Alan Watts once wrote that

> By replacing fear of the unknown with curiosity we open ourselves up to an infinite stream of possibilities. We can let fear rule our lives or we can become childlike with curiosity, pushing our boundaries, leaping out of our comfort zones, and accepting what life has put before us.[56]

Curiosity can help you rise to the intellectual demands posed by photography's realm of critical theory.

Critical theory is a domain of great thinkers' perspectives. The observations they make and the ideas they pose may be dramatically different from the way you see and understand the world. Their writings are important, because their observations can teach you about the very nature and essence of photography. According to Elizabeth Wells,

> Studying critical theory helps you to understand how meanings are generated and circulated visually. This supports your ability to communicate effectively through photography, thereby enhancing your image-making judgements and empowering you to engage within contemporary cultural issues and debates.[57]

10.4324/9781003106685-13

As Wells points out, if you are receptive, those insights can directly inform your photography practice. They can also influence the way you understand the implications of photography itself.

Critical theory presents you with what Professors Donna West Brett and Natalya Lusty describe as

> a series of complex histories alongside an equally complicated set of theoretical traditions, all of which illuminate but also sometimes confound how we understand the technological and ontological dimensions of the photographic, let alone the role of photography as a meaning-making practice.[58]

That meaning-making relates to your own work, while it also applies to the way you observe, think about, and critique images. Critical theory prepares you to recognize meaningful ideas when they appear in historical and contemporary photographs. You will see and understand photos in ways you weren't able to previously, with a more critical and discerning eye.

Artist and writer Victor Burgin explains that "Theory sets out to question the underlying assumptions of common sense in order to replace them, where necessary, with better-founded, or more comprehensive, explanations."[59] By examining photography's "underlying assumptions," you will discover new ways of evaluating your own assumptions, leading to a better understanding about the role of images in the world. The act of rethinking and re-examining can also lead to novel approaches to the ways you approach your own creative practice.

The purpose of this chapter is to offer practical tips for unpacking and extracting the information from the (sometimes dense) writings of critical theory. Many students find theoretical writing difficult to read. It might confront your usual ways of thinking, but it's worth the effort to discover a world of ideas that you've probably not encountered. This is a world of uncommon perceptions and exceptional ideas about every aspect of photography. Critical theory is important, because by exploring this world you can expand your intellectual boundaries and stimulate your mind.

Critical theory consists of writings from artists, philosophers, academics, and critics, like Susan Sontag, John Szarkowski, John Tagg, Roland Barthes, Graham Clarke, and John Berger. The writings of these theorists can introduce you to the intellectual possibilities that exist within your study of photography. And, in being introduced, the hope is that you use your mind to analyze what you read, think critically about what it means, all while formulating your own questions and conclusions.

Photographers who enjoy intellectual and philosophical approaches to photography can find critical theory exciting. It's models, concepts, and ideas serve to influence the work of many photographers, such as Robert Adams' New Topographics, and John Baldessari's use of appropriated imagery. In the same way, your consideration of critical theory may inspire a new line of photographic enquiry as part of your own practice.

Reading critical theory offers opportunities to practice and develop your critical thinking skills. Dr. Richard Paul and Dr. Linda Elder tell us that a critical thinker is someone who

- raises vital questions and problems, formulating them clearly and precisely;
- gathers and assesses relevant information, using abstract ideas to interpret it effectively;
- comes to well-reasoned conclusions and solutions, testing them against relevant criteria and standards;
- thinks open mindedly within alternative systems of thought, recognizing and assessing, as need be, their assumptions, implications, and practical consequences; and
- communicates effectively with others in figuring out solutions to complex problems.[60]

Depending on the author you are reading, there are varying levels of writing, ranging from articulate and understandable to confusing and difficult to comprehend. For example, many readers find Susan Sontag fairly accessible and Roland Barthes' writing to be almost impenetrable. Hopefully your curriculum will begin with authors on the easy end of the spectrum and help you work up toward more complex readings. When you encounter a text that's hard to understand, it may be because the writer's unique use of language can become an obstacle.

Approach these readings like you would eat a pizza: divide it into pieces and eat one bite at a time. Start by scanning over the reading and see if anything pops out that will give you a broad understanding of what this reading is about. Then try to get the gist of each paragraph. What is the author trying to communicate? If you aren't able to grasp any ideas, take a step back from the reading and find some background materials about the author. Professor of Art History, Brittni Collins suggests watching videos which break down and elaborate on how the authors think in order to get a context for what you are reading. The School of Life offers short videos that explain the perspectives of thinkers on critical theory (https://bit.ly/2bVcNyy). Professor Collins also recommends that you

1. Pay attention to how the authors use words and how they define them, because meaning can fluctuate with how they use those words, especially in reference to key concepts.
2. Talk with people who understand critical theory, and ask questions to help clarify your understanding.
3. Write an outline as you read, in order to follow the author's train of thought.
4. Try to interpret what the writers are saying while keeping in mind that readers can come to different conclusions based on their familiarity with the author and their collection of writings. Even authors of critical theory debate their own differences of interpretation.[61]

As you read more difficult texts, you may get bored, confused, and uncomfortable. If this happens, learn to recognize these feelings and pay attention to how your mind will seek out distractions in order to divert your attention away from these unpleasant feelings. If you can, limit the temptation for distractions by going to a place where there aren't any people and it's quiet enough to concentrate. Bring a drink and a snack to keep your energy up, or in case you are distracted by thirst or hunger.

It may also help to use the Pomodoro Technique. This entails giving yourself reasonable blocks of time where you focus only on reading, like a half-hour (or what's comfortable for you). Set the timer on your phone, but turn the ringer and vibrate settings off (the timer will still go off). Then, put your phone face down in front of you. This way you won't hear calls or texts or feel the anxiety of being away from your phone. When your alarm goes off, give yourself a reward. Stand up, walk around and eat that snack. Check your phone for messages in case something important has happened while you have been disconnected from the world. In five minutes, set the timer again and refocus on the reading for your next time block.[62]

Dr. Carissa Massey, Provost at Pennsylvania College of Art & Design, recommends that you

> stand and read silently or out-loud. In those cases where it's difficult to comprehend, read the text out-loud to peers in a study group. Then you should wrestle together with putting the author's ideas in your own words, translating it into everyday language. Work with other students to create an "in your own words" critical theory dictionary for the class.[63]

Sometimes critical theory can look like a foreign language. You will probably have to pick up your phone once in a while to look up words like "representational," "ontology," "semiotics," "punctum," "epistemological," "deconstruction," and "ideology" (to name a few). When you encounter a new word, try to find how the author defines the word, as opposed to only using the dictionary definition. Then, write out both the dictionary definition and the definition as used in the reading. You will probably need both of the definitions later.

Once you can understand the vocabulary, try using enquiry-based learning as a strategy for identifying important information from these valuable readings. This approach recommends formulating questions before you read, and using your problem-solving skills to find answers while you read. Having questions gives you a purpose for reading. Use this method to engage the material directly and actively while extracting the information you think is important.

Ask yourself the following five questions:

1. What is the topic (or topics) the author is exploring?
2. What does the author want me to learn?
3. Why is this reading important to my understanding of photography?
4. How can these ideas contribute to my photography practice?
5. In what ways do I agree or not agree with the author's ideas?

Call on the motivational force of your curiosity to gather the information you need to articulate the answers to your questions. If you still can't understand what the author is saying, read and reread the words and try to make sense of the ideas the author is trying to convey. Give yourself permission to slow down and read one sentence at a time, to help increase your comprehension. Affirm for yourself what you understand from what you've read by saying it out loud. After you finish each paragraph, write a sentence or two that summarizes, in your own words, the big idea in that paragraph. Keep in mind that this isn't like reading a novel. This is a slow, methodical kind of reading that requires practice and patience.

When you finish the reading, look back at your outline, summaries, and your responses to the questions listed above. Think about your intellectual reactions to the author's ideas. Do you find their ideas interesting? Are there points you agree with? Do you disagree with anything the author proposed? If so, why? Next, what did you learn about yourself from the way you read the text? Did you find you could understand it? Did you need to use some of the suggested strategies to make your way through the reading? If your mind sought distractions, how did you handle them?

If you make an honest attempt to complete the reading, and find that your reading skill level is preventing you from accessing the material, ask your instructor for advice. You could also ask for professional summaries or use other campus resources that can provide help.

Once you are able to access the writing, you might encounter ideas that you connect with, along with ideas that you feel are completely foreign to your way of thinking. The point is to try to understand the author's arguments, think critically about their perspectives, and see if what they say has any correlation to your own understanding of photography, especially your photography practice. Try to be open to expanding your own understanding with these writings. Finally, consider what these theories have to teach and how they may help you generate new ideas.

Part 4
Create

14

The Photographer's Brain – A User Manual

Your most important piece of photo equipment is something money can't buy. It's your brain! It is a complex biological instrument that does all the work of seeing, processing, interpreting, recognizing, analyzing, and identifying what you perceive. It's the original camera. Your brain captures images all the time, storing them in short- and long-term memory. The theory behind this chapter is that, if you understand how your brain works, you'll be able to use it better as a tool for expressing your creative ideas and capturing your unique vision.

The first thing you need to know is that your brain, a photographer's brain, isn't like other brains. When you capture photos you really like, it experiences enjoyment and pleasure. It's that feeling of looking into your camera's preview screen and feeling happy. That sensation provides positive reinforcement by way of a brain-chemical reward process. The happy feeling makes you want to take more photos! It compels you to seek out more psychological and emotional self-rewards.

Another phenomenon that comes into play is called *optimistic bias*. Optimistic bias is when your brain believes that the photos you make in the future will be more exciting than the ones you made today.[64] In other words, your brain thinks that there is a very high chance that you can take more successful photos today than the most successful images you made yesterday. When you take those photos today, you may not like them as much as tomorrow's photos! It is a self-perpetuating cycle of hope and optimism!

10.4324/9781003106685-14

Another mental strategy is that, if you experience a feeling of dissatisfaction with your images, it can motivate you to think of new ways to approach your photography practice, to think up novel ideas as ways to reach your expectations. Consider how quickly your mind can change from "This is an amazing shot," to "I can make a photo that's better than this one," or "None of my photos are any good." Because satisfaction is fleeting, you anticipate how trying again could produce better results. Some human brains tend to try again and again until it's able to meet or exceed the intended results. Other brains want to give up. Those that stick with photography tend to want to push forward. Regardless of whether or not you get the result you want, it makes you try even harder to capture a photo that gives you pleasure. You can see this tendency in photographers, golfers, gamers, and even people who buy lottery tickets!

Your brain knows that the joy of photography is something that happens through the journey *and* at the destination. The journey is understood to be the entire creative process of making images. The destination is the pleasure you feel when you capture photos that are successful enough to put in your portfolio. Your brain gets a rush of satisfaction when you are able to make a composition that you think looks amazing. At the most basic level, you make photos because your brain enjoys it.

These supportive neurological processes don't only happen when you make images. They also happen when you see other people's interesting, attractive, and engaging photos. For example, when you look at photos by one of your favorite artists, they make you feel good, you feel a connection, and that inspires you. Seeing a photo that stimulates your mind has an impact. You experience feelings of happiness. When you emotionally or psychologically relate to a photo, it's evidence that a photographer was able to communicate something with an image, which reached out and awoke something within you. Connecting with a photo can make your brain feel exhilarated!

As a photographer, your brain uses your eyes to visually isolate areas within a scene, separating it from the whole of its surroundings. Your brain methodically interprets its environs and tries to find meaning from the visual stimuli. It does this in part by using the eyes to seek patterns in its 180-degree field of view. It's compelled to identify visible elements, to understand what it sees. Your brain constantly looks for information to organize and structure into meaning.

Your neurological framework is attracted to contrast, colors, light, shadow, and the way those things communicate a sense of texture, form, depth, and dimension. Your perception is also naturally drawn toward faces, eyes, and things shaped like circles. The colors red and yellow grab your brain's attention. Remember your brain's natural tendencies when you include these elements in your compositions. For example, putting a red stop sign in the middle of your photo will bring the viewer's eyes to the center, leaving all the other areas of the composition to suffer, because the colorful, circular object will dominate the viewer's attention.

When two objects are near each other, your brain presumes there is a meaningful relationship between those things and tries to understand how these things relate. Sometimes, after it identifies a logical reason, your brain comes up with alternative, illogical meanings based on information from memories. These stored resources help the brain invent creative, sometimes irrational, solutions for what else visual relationships could mean. The resulting conclusion could be seen as a creative idea. Such a method of problem solving is possible because your brain has the capacity to use all its resources to think creatively. You have a natural neurological capacity for creativity.

To help explain how memory and creativity work together, here is an analogy that I call "Greenhouses in the Backyard of Your Brain." Imagine that your memories are collected in your head and kept in small, glass-paned greenhouses in the backyard of your brain. Imagine your memories are stored and nourished in these greenhouses. These are the places that memories either live and thrive or fade away. The more you retrieve (remember) them, the stronger and more available they become.

When you want to recall a memory, you just follow the little path to that greenhouse, open the door, and there it is: a holographic description of that recollection. It could be a memory of when you made your first photograph. Or, it could be a memory of feeling happy while being praised by your instructor for how ingenious one of your images was.

Imagine that there are billions of these greenhouses in your brain. When you want to remember the name of the French inventor of photography, you think about the memory you are looking for, you go down the appropriate path, pass through that door, and encounter the memory of Nicéphore Niépce. And, the more you walk a path, the more established the path becomes, and the easier it will be to find that memory next time.

When you want to achieve a creative goal, your mind looks for any memory that could be associated with that goal. It leads your attention down many paths to gain access to all the greenhouses with memories that are most likely to relate to the request for an idea. If your brain can find the right path, then it can retrieve the memory in that greenhouse.

The interesting thing about the brain is that these greenhouses aren't arranged in an organized way. One greenhouse containing the memory of a photo you saw of a Colorado mountain range by Ansel Adams could be next to another that holds a memory of giant air balloons floating across the sky. Another greenhouse could contain an old memory of the tree in the backyard of your best friend's home. As you try to remember, you might also gain access to a few recent memories about water issues in the Great Lakes and the peas you ate for dinner last night. Then, in a creative flash, all the neurons connect and you collect a mashup of memories that produce an idea like Jerry Uelsmann's photograph *Floating Tree*.

The number of greenhouses in the brain and the memories they hold are different for every person. This is because everyone's life experiences are different. If you are an 18- to 22-year-old, then your life experiences are very different from someone who is 65, has traveled the world, worked every day of their adult life, and has raised a couple of kids. The older person has accumulated a greater diversity of memories, yet both of you have your own particular worldview, beliefs, and interests that will contribute to the creation of photographs about particular topics that interest each of you.

If you are a young person and you are having a hard time accessing the memories you need to generate a creative idea, then you can try brainstorming. This method can help you access memories by associating one idea with another. The way brainstorming works is this. You access a memory greenhouse and then explore all the surrounding greenhouses, then memories combine that help generate unfiltered ideas that relate to the creative challenges you are working on. In the process, you identify sensory (visual) or conceptual associations between memories. Multiple memories can arise when they share some kind of relationship. It's like using hashtags on Instagram to look for related topics.

For example, let's say you are working on a photo project that has to do with anxiety and you want to come up with ideas around that word. Your mind will search for memories associated with that word. It will recall stressful events, emotions, and the faces of people you know who suffer from anxiety. The amazing thing that happens in the process is that the creative mind will also access some of those other memory greenhouses that are in proximity to memories of anxiety, formulating completely new, unique ideas.

In this analogy for how creativity works, you can see that memories are valuable resources that support and fuel your capacity for creativity. Your life experiences not only shape the way you perceive the world, they are also the raw material you need to generate creative ideas. So, when your instructor recommends you *think outside the box*, your mind's greenhouses may be the boxes they are talking about!

All the experiences in your life have brought you to this moment. You never know how what you learned from those experiences will lay the groundwork for future experiences. After all, your life is the sum total of the memories that came from experiences you've accumulated. Creative work relies on you being able to access those memories to express ideas in unique, unconventional, and innovative ways. It would stand to reason that the more memorable experiences you collect, the more material you will have to make those creative mental connections. And remember: it's not just about how many memories you have, but also the quality and impact those memories had on you. Let's study this further in the next chapter.

15

Your Creative Mind

It's exciting to learn about creativity, because everything you learn can be used to dream up something that never existed before! Creativity can inspire you to act in unpredictable and sometimes risky ways. It dares you to take a chance, to experiment without knowing what will happen! It asks you to be open to the unknown, while staying curious about how your mind will answer the question "What if?" For instance, what if you ask a stranger to come into the studio for a photo session? What if you convert that color photo to black and white? What if you are courageous enough to take a chance with your assignment, if for no other reason than because you are curious to see how it will turn out? Find that place inside you that asks, "What would that look like in a photograph?" Or "What would it look like if I did this?" Then promise yourself to find out.

Poet Dorothy Parker tells us that the other cure for boredom is curiosity, pointing out that "There is no cure for curiosity." Inquisitiveness is an impulse that can trigger and awaken your brain's creative energies. It generates a sense of purpose with feelings of anticipation and expectation. Become interested in what would happen if you overcome your fear of failing and take the photo anyway. Curiosity and creativity are natural, dynamic aspects of your inventive mind. Use them to motivate yourself, to try something new.

As mentioned in the previous chapter, sometimes thinking creatively is described as "thinking outside the box." In this metaphor the box is actually understood to be self-imposed limits, the habit of settling for the same conventional ideas that everyone comes up with. When thinking outside the box, you are able to see challenges from new perspectives and, in turn, solve

DOI: 10.4324/9781003106685-15

problems with uncommon, unconventional solutions. Studies on the human brain tell us that everyone has the power to be creative. Everyone has a creative impulse. We all have the ability to think of novel, one-of-a-kind approaches that are uniquely suited to solve seemingly unsolvable problems.

If you doubt whether or not you can be creative, think about your own capacity to dream while you are asleep (assuming you can remember your dreams). Your mind can invent fantastical creatures, nightmarish characters, and give you magical abilities like flying! Dreams are evidence that the human brain has the power to interpret and transform what it perceives in endless creative ways. Your creative mind is free to play when you are asleep, and dreams are examples of some of the most artistic, surreal practices that a photographer's brain performs. There is no human activity that is more creative than the mind's ability to compose stories from apparently unrelated memories. Your dreams prove that your power to think creatively is as common as the stars in the night sky.

A creative mind is receptive and persistent enough to generate original ideas, unique ways of seeing, and/or imaginative interpretations. When new ideas arrive, it seems like magic. It's like your muse has just answered your prayer (and maybe they did). The whole process seems mysterious, but ideas are actually explainable results from your brain's naturally functioning neurophysiology. It seems somewhat mysterious, but it's something you are capable of developing and exercising to enrich your photography practice.

The antithesis of creativity is the "right" answer. For example, when you solve a math problem, there is one right answer. Every other solution is incorrect. In contrast, there is a wide spectrum of possible solutions for every artistic problem. Some are better than others, but none of them is the "right" answer. Your challenge is to find the best possible idea using the resources you have (material, time, and energy), within the parameters you are given.

Creativity is an expressive energy that can be made to flow by going through the stages referred to here as Develop, Stop, Insight, and Evaluate. You will learn about this process in the next chapter. Much of the process has to do with purposefully struggling to generate an idea, a solution to a problem. During such a mental exercise – which can take two seconds, two days, or two weeks – the synapses sparking in your brain might find just the right paths that lead to great ideas.

The creative struggle opens the mind to unrealized possibilities, but it can be frustrating. You can endure the frustration of the process by holding on to your sense of curiosity and focusing on your desire for an answer, your need to discover a unique solution. It can be difficult, but it's worth it. It can cause you to feel a bit anxious, but, as T. S. Eliot once said, "Anxiety is the handmaiden to creativity."[65] It may feel uncomfortable, but it can result in the pleasurable experience of reward: an exciting, inspiring, original idea! Generating new ideas can strengthen your creative confidence and bring fresh energy and enthusiasm to your photo practice. Take a risk. Try to stay open to the experiences of anticipation, uncertainty, and, eventually you will find the successes of creativity.

If you find that your mind is delivering thoughts like "I can't think of anything. I don't want to struggle to find ideas. I don't like my photos. Why am I doing this?" or "My photographs aren't good enough," then try to recognize that these thoughts are just thoughts. They aren't even true! These self-judgments are your brain's response to the creative challenge, and lots of people, to some degree, think these things about themselves. Even accomplished photographers sometimes have these thoughts! The difference between novices and masterful photographers, in this regard, is that the experts don't let these inner voices stop them from picking up their camera and heading out the door to make photos. What's important to remember is this is a natural part of the process, so don't let these thoughts slow you down on your creative journey!

It's easy to get into a habit of using familiar and typical artistic solutions instead of going beyond your comfort zone to try something different. Creative thinking requires being willing to take risks. Regularly give yourself permission to take risks and even to fail. It's OK to feel disappointed with your work. Everyone does, sometimes. Lots of famous makers and inventors have suggested that there is no such thing as failure. Failure is just the opportunity to learn what doesn't work.

Failing, every once in a while, in your photo practice is necessary in order to arrive at the images that are successful. For example, photographer Willem Vrey said that, in his experience,

> 1 out of 100 shots are decent and may be good enough to use in most situations. Maybe 1 in 5000 shots are very good, and probably 1 out of every 100,000 shots (for me about 1 per year) are good enough to build a serious career and reputation on.[66]

I think Vrey would agree that, if you aren't failing often, you are failing to reach your creative photographic potential!

When you're making photos in a habitual, comfortable way, then consciously do something else. Sure, go ahead and stand in the place that every other photographer stands and make that photo that everyone has posted on Instagram. But then try a different approach, something that you wouldn't normally try. Move to a new location or lie on the ground to change your vantage point. Your creative mind benefits from "cultivating divergent thinking skills and deliberately exposing ourselves to new experiences and to learning."[67] The more you practice taking the idea one step further, the more ideas will come.

Sometimes the volume of a creative idea gets loud enough to move your body to action. Hopefully you respond with a sense of curiosity that will stimulate your creative mind. Stay conscious of your photography habits and push yourself to go beyond them. By practicing this method over and over, you can change an uncreative habit into a creative habit. The more attention you show your creative practice, the more it will reward you.

Creative ideas can come during any phase of the photo-making process. "Creativity is associated with many factors, including conducive environments, ideal collaborators, personality traits, serendipity, and even a quest for spiritual muses."[68] Pre-production, production, and post-production are packed with opportunities for ideas and unexpected creative surprises. Some surprises can seem disappointing, especially when the surprise yields a result you didn't expect. But, at second glance, you might be thrilled to see that, at second glance, it's something you really like! This is called a "happy accident."

For example, let's say you are standing in a street, composing a photo of an open doorway. The scene is interesting because of the colors of the house, and there are two dogs lying on the ground, one on either side of the door. Then, just as you are about to push the shutter release, a woman wearing a red dress walks across the doorway from the inside of the house, taking the visual impact of this image from good to great! This is what happened to Susan Meiselas as she was making a photo in Nicaragua in 1971. That unforeseen entrance of the woman ended up helping Meiselas to make a world-renowned image, that was included in her book *Nicaragua*.[69]

Another way you can boost your creativity is by forming your own creative support network (CSN). Think of this as a dream team of people you can brainstorm with, who can offer ideas for projects you are working on, and who can help you see aspects of your work from angles that you can't see. What if your CSN was made of photographers, but also included a sculptor, a painter, a graphic designer, a ceramicist, an art historian, and even a creative writer? Think of the variety of perspectives and ideas that could happen with this kind of support team. Since you are likely living in a place that has all of these kinds of people (an academic campus), you should be able to bring together a valuable group. Make it a reciprocal arrangement. For your group members, offer the same kind of feedback, ideas, and support when they are deep in the creative struggle.

The next resources of inspiration can come from two sources: *living role models*, and what photographer Philip Ringler calls *ghost mentors*. Your living role models (mentors) can be teachers, instructors, professors, and professionals who have worked closely with you to foster growth in your practice and are willing to help you reach your photography goals. For many students, these people are photographers and/or photography instructors. They could also be talented, competent artists and teachers from other disciplines.

A mentor is someone you aspire to be like, that you respect, and who serves as an exemplar. They are someone who has a history of making creative work that inspires you or whose degree of expertise or wisdom impresses you. Photographer Bruce Dorn recommends that a mentor be someone that reinforces "the positive results while cutting plenty of slack for inevitable errors." He says a mentor should

> Be realistic about [their] expectations and remember to point out missteps as well. Criticism, even well-intentioned and very mild criticism, can cut to the quick of a beginner's confidence, so [mentors should] err on the side of kindness … we're not handing out participation trophies here, we're being thoughtful and supportive.[70]

Last, a mentor is someone that is willing to listen to your ideas, look at your work, offer meaningful feedback, and engage with you in conversation about the most productive directions to take with your photography. Their actions should challenge you to be more creative and help more deeply awaken your creative impulse. Their words should transmit a sense of confidence in your artistic choices.

Ghost mentors, on the other hand, aren't physically available. They still fit some of the descriptions of the living mentor, but with them you find advice and inspiration through records of their past words and works. Ghost mentors could be people like Susan Sontag, Roland Barthes, John Szarkowski, Jo Spence, or Gisèle Freund. The wisdom of these people's observations, thoughts, and ideas could serve as fuel for your creative engine. They can cause you to think in ways that energize your creative process. Their advice can challenge your intellectual limits in a way that can help you see ideas about your projects in new ways. To help keep your connection to your ghost mentors active, try reading them on occasion, listen to past interviews, or watch videos. Look at and absorb impressions from their works of art. It also helps to keep photos of them on your desk, stuck on your refrigerator, or pinned to a wall in your studio.

The point here is to take advantage of every creative resource at your disposal in order to support your photography practice, including all those artists whose work you admire. By putting together and participating in a CSN, it nurtures your creative abilities. Surround yourself with inspired thinkers and artworks that are the products of artistic brilliance. Take advantage of your external resources and you will awaken the creative resources that are inside you.

16

Cultivate Your Creativity

Creativity is one of your mind's active principles. It's an abundant resource. Author and poet Maya Angelou once said, "You can't use up creativity. The more you use, the more you have."[71] When you tap this incredible resource, new ideas awaken a complex series of neurological events that happen across your whole brain. A cascade of firing neurons reaches out to access memories, emotions, your conscious and unconscious mind. In your brain's right and left hemispheres, a chemical-electrical network searches for and finds the resources it needs to formulate previously unknown solutions and innovative ways of seeing and understanding. Step by step, the process unfolds until the light bulb comes on over your head, powered by the energy of a new idea!

Artists, writers, scientists, and philosophers have tried to break down the creative process as a series of defined steps, from the beginning to the end product. In truth, there isn't a definitive, step-by-step sequence for every situation. Yet this chapter attempts to break down the creative activity into four stages, where you Develop, Stop, gain Insight, and Evaluate your ideas. This process, much like other theoretical, step-by-step descriptions, happens sometimes but not every time. On occasion, there is no progression of steps, or warning. Ideas can spontaneously appear!

As a long-term investment in your creative process, plan on collecting lots of memory resources that will help you generate ideas. Memories are the sustenance for your creative mind. Beat writers from the 1950s believed that there was an essential rule of creativity, "We *need* new and unusual experiences to think differently. In fact, cultivating a mind-set that is open and explorative

10.4324/9781003106685-16

might be the best thing we can do for our creative work." The author goes on to say that "Any life experience-whether traumatic or ecstatic-that diversifies our repertoire of experiences and pushes us outside of habitual thought patterns can lead us to enhanced cognitive flexibility and creativity."[72]

Try new things. Tinder executive Brian Norgard advises that if you want to unlock your creativity, you should "slow down, study another field, get into nature, get out of office, music (lots), sketch, cardio before/after, nibble on small ideas, throw stuff away, atomize the work, look for orthogonal inspiration, breathe, learn about circadian rhythm, paint."[73] New activities provide additional memories that you might use later as part of your photography practice. Whatever memories you have are a unique collection of life experiences that no one else could possibly have. Thus, the innovative solutions you come up with will be truly unique. Here is a four-step theory for how it all comes together to produce results: Develop, Stop, Insight, and Evaluate.

1. DEVELOP

It all begins with the desire for an idea, concept, solution, a resolution to an unreasonable artistic challenge. Development is the process of drawing out an idea that is somewhere in the darkness. It is the friction between the emotions of frustration and anticipation that supplies the energy needed to arrive at creative solutions. B. J. Cary recommends you to:

> Dig deep here. Allow yourself to get worked up to a point where you really *feel* that fire of frustration burning you inside. Wake up that anguish, anxiety, insecurity, or frustration … Clench your fists. Stomp your feet. Hop up and down. Whatever you need to do, get that fire burning HOT![74]

Yes, ideas emerge from frustration.

As this energy grows, it focuses your brain's attention, activating and sorting through a wide variety of memories, to find combinations of experiences that have the potential to formulate an unimagined composite of ideas. This is how an idea gestates, then comes to life as a result of your brain solving the puzzle! How long it will take for your brain to deliver a workable idea is anybody's guess. There is no timetable - it takes as long as it takes.

The emergence of a creative idea is unpredictable and can appear in your thoughts at any time! When concepts start trickling in, *pay attention to them*. Write them down, so you won't forget. The more attention you place on emerging ideas, the better the process will work for you. If you stay open and engaged with developing thoughts, more ideas can emerge, leading to the project's full creative maturity. But ideas can't manifest unless you take the actions needed to help them take form.

Sustain focus on the problem. Give creativity enough time to deliver a result. There can be a degree of obsession with this step. If you don't sustain your directed focus, you will never gain the momentum necessary for ideas to emerge in the next steps. How long should you stay focused? Until it yields a result. Neuroscientist Jonah Lehrer says that

> feeling frustration – the act of being stumped – is an essential part of the creative process. Before we can find the answer – before we probably even know the question – we must be immersed in disappointment, convinced that a solution is beyond our reach. We need to have wrestled with the problem and lost … It's often at this point, *after* we've stopped searching for the answer, that the answer arrives.[75]

Because frustration is uncomfortable, your brain may find it difficult to hold attention for very long. As a result, your mind might try to divert your attention by seeking distraction. A voice in your head will whisper, "Hey, someone must have texted me. I'll check." Or "I'm hungry. I need a snack." Or "I'm bored. I'll think about this later." As it turns out, occasional distractions aren't always counterproductive. Sometimes it helps to stop, and shift of focus can help your brain formulate ideas. How often you alternate between frustration and distractions is up to you. Over time, you'll come to know what works for you.

2. STOP

After you have struggled with the idea for a while, consciously stop thinking about it and redirect your attention on something else (as mentioned above). Shift your thoughts to other things. When you do, your brain will continue to work on the problem. It will carry on sorting through memories, searching for experiences that might be able to help invent a solution. Think of this process as having an online search engine open in a background tab, looking for hits on your requested topic. Instead of using the web, you are using your neural network. Instead of searching websites, your brain is searching through your memories. You just have to give it time to respond. Graham Wallas calls this stage "incubation," where ideas are allowed to formulate, solidify, and evolve into ideas that can be considered as solutions to the problem.[76] Rely on your brain's ability to locate the resources it needs to overcome the challenge. Don't give up, stay engaged, and let the process unfold.

3. INSIGHT

If everything goes well, you will generate insights and solutions on your idea quest. Insights can come at any time. It's somewhat common for people to have ideas in dreams. For example, in 1869, Russian Chemist Dmitri Mendeleev ended a multi-year search for a way to classify and organize chemical elements. While asleep, he recalled: "I saw in a dream, a table, where all the elements fell into place as required. Awakening, I immediately wrote it down on a piece of paper."[77] Thus, the periodic table of elements was created.

4. EVALUATE

Not all the ideas that come out of this process are workable, usable ideas. Beware of concepts that come quickly or easily, because they may be inferior solutions masquerading as exceptional inspirations. Sometimes the mind will provide a quick suggestion based on common memories, like going to class, eating lunch, going out with friends, or watching the sun go down. This kind of idea could be an overused and clichéd solution. If you don't recognize it for what it is, your classmates may point it out during critique.

You may find yourself in a situation where you need photos for your assignment and the landmarks at your college seem like really good subjects. The trouble with this idea is that countless photo students before you have come up with the same solution and your instructor has been inundated with those subjects over the years. When you rethink this course of action, it turns out not to be an original idea. When something like this happens, push past that idea and keep up the pressure for something more imaginative and innovative. Make space for new ideas to emerge and, when they do, evaluate them for their level of creativity and practicality.

Mendeleev struggled for years to get a breakthrough on his inventions and ingenious chemistry ideas. In contrast, you have assignment deadlines. You can't afford to take weeks, let alone years, to produce an idea. Your time constraints are very real and your instructors want you to meet their deadlines. You'll never be able to use the excuse "I don't have the assignment finished because I'm still incubating in the *stop* phase."

If you feel creatively stuck, you can take a more proactive approach. Try using the *Blockbuster cards,* which are challenges loosely based on Brian Eno and Peter Schmidt's Oblique Strategies cards.[78] Blockbusters present random creative challenges that help you move away from whatever creative block you're experiencing by guiding you into another, parallel, creative dilemma. The idea is that your brain is forced to stop and temporarily redirect your attention onto a different challenge.

The cards work best during a creative crisis, yet they also work well in other stages of the creative process. Start by getting a partner and draw one card. Work together to interpret the challenge. You could also draw two cards and figure out how the statements relate to each other. You *must* commit to come up with an in-depth response, no matter how frustrating the journey may be. You should each contribute to the response by trying to figure out what you should do to respond. Start with discussing what you think the card is looking for, then brainstorm ideas to get to the best reply. The more deeply you consider what the card says, and the more sincere your response, the better the cards will work to awaken your creative mind. Complete these actions:

1. *Question*. What challenge is posed by the card?
2. Consider. Figure out how what the card says relates to you.
3. *Solution*. How will you respond to the challenge?

Brian Eno said that his cards

> evolved from me being in a number of working situations when the panic of the situation – particularly in [music] studios – tended to make me quickly forget that there were other ways of working and that there were tangential ways of attacking problems that were in many senses more interesting than the direct head-on approach. If you're in a panic, you tend to take the head-on approach because it seems to be the one that's going to yield the best results. Of course, that often isn't the case – it's just the most obvious and – apparently – reliable method. The function of the Oblique Strategies was, initially, to serve as a series of prompts which said, "Don't forget that you could adopt *this* attitude," or "Don't forget you could adopt *that* attitude."[79]

Blockbusters work in much the same way, to nudge you out of your habitual ways of finding ideas by activating a thought process called *lateral thinking*, which Wikipedia defines as "a manner of solving problems using an indirect and creative approach via reasoning that is not immediately obvious. It involves ideas that may not be obtainable using only traditional step-by-step logic."[80]

This method helps you see other vantage points from which you can think about creative challenges. Use the cards to stimulate your brain as it continues to work on your primary creative challenge in the background of your consciousness. A set of cards is included on the website at www.photostudent.net> Resources > Blockbusters. You can print them and cut them out for your own use.

In addition to the Blockbuster cards, here is another fun, creative exercise you can do with your classmates. Think of as many uses for a digital photograph as you can in 15 minutes. Now, how many uses can you think of for a photographic print in the same amount of time? Try to let your creative thoughts flow – unobstructed, while actively avoiding conventional, clichéd thinking.

Neuroscientists believe that, the more you practice generating creative ideas, the better your brain gets at searching for and compiling data for a response. In other words, the more you practice creative thinking, the more creative you become. When your confidence in your creative abilities grows, you can establish a habitual way of functioning creatively. Creativity can then emerge in other aspects of your life. Regularly, you will begin to see your world through creative eyes and that will transform the way you think of and practice photography.

17

Creative Possibilities

The creative photographer is forever finding new ways to interpret the world. Their photos capture things viewers may have never seen with their own eyes! Using the imagination, photographers can show viewers things that never existed. The photographer can dream up and create visual worlds that would never be possible if it weren't for the remarkable capabilities of the human brain. It's this potential your instructor is trying to awaken in you when they give an assignment. Assignments are designed to be challenges, arguments that are asking for your thoughtful, ingenious response. Knowing this, how will you respond to the assigned challenges?

There are several times where creativity comes into play during the production of your assignment. To awaken your potential for creative ideas, it can help if you understand when the possibility for innovative ideas is the greatest. There are seven optimal points during your pre-production, production, and post-production workflow when you can apply creative insights, original ideas, and innovative solutions.

1. CONCEPT

The time you spend developing your concept is ripe with creative potential. When you come up with special ideas for your project, be open and allow your ideas to change and evolve throughout the production stage. There is a

10.4324/9781003106685-17

difference between theoretical ideas and practice. The things you *theorize* will happen during the making of your photos may be very different than what actually happens during production. Allow for unexpected events and situations to influence your creative process. You can never be certain about what will happen. Music composer Julie Burnstein advises that, "Whatever we can do to expand our capacity for uncertainty, that's a wonderful preparation for creativity."[81] The mindset with which you approach your photography workflow should be "intention with flexibility and spontaneity."

If your intention is to do street photography, prepare by going where something interesting is most likely to happen. When you're in position, be ready to spontaneously respond to your surroundings. Part of your strategy is to be hypervigilant, to be intentionally aware, so, when the unguarded moment presents itself, you are prepared and ready to make the capture. As Louis Pasteur once said, "chance favors the prepared mind."

There is a lot of chance involved in street photography, but for every photographic venture there are ways to improve the likelihood of getting successful photos. Your odds will always be better if you make a plan and consider some creative ideas before you set out with your camera. A skillful photographer prepares by researching to find the locations with highest photogenic potential. In the same way an experienced fisherman knows the best places on the lake to catch fish. It doesn't mean they will definitely catch fish, but knowing where to go will make success more likely.

Some artistic concepts require more elaborate planning, like building tableau scenes in the studio. Lori Nix would probably agree that, to realize a photographic vision, you will need sketches, building supplies, maybe a model or other photographic subjects, and a lot of time to carry out your plan. All the logistics, supplies, and equipment for the shoot need to be carefully considered ahead of time. Success for this kind of approach relies on comprehensive planning.

If one of the topics you are interested in is climate change, social justice, or personal freedom, then pre-visualized concepts can evolve during planning. Bear in mind that every idea you have is subject to change, abandonment, or transformation. Many photographers rely on creativity as part of their concept – for example, Francesca Woodman, Hans Bellmer, Shirin Neshat, Yinka Shonibare, Miles Aldridge, Paul Outerbridge, and Yevonde Middleton.

When it comes down to it, you only have two options for your approach to photography. You either have to get in front of subjects that will make visually interesting photos, or you will have to elevate common, unremarkable subjects in ways that make their qualities appear remarkable.

Whatever subject or genre you choose to work with, use your photographic tools, unique vision, and sense of purpose to make photos that express how you perceive the subject matter. Take what interests you and make images that elaborate on, enhance, and transform what you see into what you want others to see. Whatever approach you take, work toward a finished product that shows viewers the remarkable way *you* see the subject.

2. EQUIPMENT

The second point where you can apply creative insights, original ideas, and innovative solutions concerns the equipment you use and how you use it. Your camera and lens choice will affect the visual qualities of your final images. You need the right tool for the job. The camera and lens you choose should be determined by how the visual qualities produced by those tools best support your concept. Do you need a lens that will yield a shallow depth of field? Or do you want a moody, atmospheric effect that a pinhole camera or a plastic Holga lens is known for? The choice is up to you. Photographers who relied on their equipment as creative tools include Lucas Samaras, Elsa Dorfman, Gordon Parks, Alfred Eisenstaedt, Craig Barber, and Miroslav Tichý.

3. LIGHT

The way you use light is an essential creative choice. Along with subject matter, light is the most important visual aspect of your photography. Even if you photograph outdoors in sunlight, plan for how best to control the available light to support your concept and subject. If you want to convey a sense of mood, drama, or atmosphere, consider how you can modify light to achieve those goals. Here are a few of the many photographers that are considered masterful in their use of light: Edward Weston, Richard Avedon, Robert Mapplethorpe, Eikoh Hosoe, Joel Meyerowitz, and Fan Ho.

4. VANTAGE POINT

This refers to where you put the camera in relationship to the subject. Your choice of camera position will influence arrangement of elements in your composition. Use your vantage point to decide where to position your main subject in relationship to all other elements in the scene. Importantly, decide how you will integrate the background into the composition. Don't ignore your background, or it becomes an area that gets filled with things that distract and visually compete with your subject matter. A distracting background is the number one element that can destroy the quality of a composition.

Vantage point also allows you to change the appearance of the lighting on the subject, whether it's a building, tree, or person. When you move, you change the visual relationship between the light source, the subject, and the camera. Your vantage point should support your creative objectives. Approach your photo session with ideas about vantage points, but also take the time to explore a variety of other camera positions. Search for unexpected possibilities, like taking a shot from the ground or shooting blindly by raising the camera high over your head. For inspiration, here are some examples of photographers who have used unconventional vantage points: Margaret Bourke-White, Charles Clyde Ebbets, Edward Burtynsky, William Eggleston, Alexander Rodchenko.

5. TIMING

Timing refers to when you choose to push the shutter release. Timing is essential when you are photographing moving subjects. Good timing is a combination of awareness and the ability to anticipate when something is about to happen. A good sense of timing allows you to show your subject in a way that the eye is incapable of seeing. This translates into using long and/or fast shutter speeds to express a sense of motion. Sports photographers, photojournalists, and wildlife photographers need to have impeccable timing to be successful. French photographer Henri Cartier-Bresson was a master of choosing the right moment to make his exposures, which he referred to as the *decisive moment.*

John Suler defines Cartier-Bresson's idea of the decisive moment as "when the visual and psychological elements of people in a real life scene spontaneously and briefly come together in perfect resonance to express the essence of that situation."[82] Check out the work of other photographers whose work stresses the importance of timing: Alfred Eisenstaedt, Eadweard Muybridge, Nick Ut, Robert Frank, Sam Shere, and Philippe Halsman.

6. CRITICAL FOCUS

The human eye is attracted to areas in a composition that are visually sharp. Knowing this emphasizes how important it is to choose where you place your critical focus and depth of field in a scene. Use creative intention to place where you want your viewer's attention to immediately land in your composition. Your use of critical focus and depth of field not only attracts, but guides, your viewer's eye through a composition, thus controlling their attention span. In addition, you choose where the focus gradually tapers off in front of and behind the subject.

7. POST-PRODUCTION CREATIVITY

There are two points where post-production can provide opportunities for your creative expression. The first is during editing, when a lot of creative magic happens. Adobe Lightroom and/or Adobe Photoshop can liberate the imaginative mind! Your workflow during editing is marked by a series of creative decisions. The great thing about editing is that you have the freedom to experiment while being able to undo any choice you make. You can ask "What if ...?" and get the answer immediately, with the option to undo immediately! It's the perfect place to take creative risks and see what else your photos could look like. Many photographers rely on post-production editing, where they can let their creative genius come alive! Here are examples of some of those photographers: Maggie Taylor, Kim Joon, Anthony Goicolea, Brooke Shaden, and Erik Johansson.

The second part of post-production creativity has to do with the end product. Photo files may be posted online or printed as physical artifacts. There are many different printing processes to consider, each providing their own distinct visual qualities. Some of these processes are inkjet, giclée, photogravure, cyanotype, and wet plate collodion. Decide which process and method of output will best support the story in your photos. For creative printing possibilities, take a look at these photographers: Ian Ruhter, Jill Enfield, Dan Burkholder, Jerry Spagnoli, Stephen Berkman, Dan Estabrook, and Binh Danh.

There are also other options for final products that involve physically making or fabricating your photographs. This includes hand building, manual compositing, collage, montage, and/or multimedia. Some photographers choose to paint on their prints. Some use images as part of sculptural installations. This is what photography author Robert Hirsch refers to as "transformational imagemaking."[83] Take a look at the work of these photographers for examples: Robert Heinecken, Joyce Neimanas, Douglas Prince, Thomas Barrow, Robert W. Fichter, Holly Roberts, Betty Hahn, Tatana Kellner, Bea Nettles, Mike and Doug Starn, and Martha Madigan.

In the art world, there are no rules for how you make your photos. It can be daunting to know there are limitless possibilities for how you apply creative insights, original ideas, and innovative solutions. There are no confining boundaries for your creativity! You might be tempted to take an easy path, an approach that's been overdone and clichéd. Or, instead, you could set out to make a new path in the realm of photography by being risky and breaking the rules of your assignment. You might even choose to photograph something in a way it's never been photographed or do something that's never been done. Be curious and explore what those ideas might look like.

Think about what you can do to keep your photo practice fresh and exciting. If you feel challenged by your instructor to make work that is unique, to break new ground, go ahead and embrace the challenge. You might feel frustrated by the unpredictability of the outcome. In the end, you may also be happy, because you will have attained a deeply enjoyable experience from finding a unique solution to your creative problem. When faced with a decision for what you should do, try sacrificing your sense of contentment and choose the path of uncertainty, of creative possibility!

18

Superpowers Need Superfuels!

Let's begin with the premise that one of your superpowers is creativity, even if it's a power you are just starting to develop. And let's assume that you want your brain to have the best possible fuel so it can reach a level of energy that helps you maximize your superpower potential. The brain needs resources to generate new ideas, to solve technical and aesthetic puzzles. This chapter is about how to take advantage of and apply the most valuable, beneficial high-octane fuel for your photography … right now!

The way you get the kind of brain energy described above is by looking at and absorbing images made by historic and contemporary photo masters. You could also look at creative works in other media, like graphic design, painting, printmaking, or sculpture. Allow yourself to be inspired and motivated by these artworks. These artists are – or were – likely more talented, more skilled, and more visually perceptive than you. And part of what brought them to this level of achievement was that they were willing to be influenced by the lessons taught by examples of other great artists. For instance, here are a few renowned photographers that studied the images made by other artists and were influenced their work:

- Diane Arbus was inspired by Lisette Model.
- Paul Strand was influenced by Alfred Stieglitz.
- Annie Leibovitz is motivated by Cartier-Bresson, Robert Frank, and Richard Avedon.
- Cindy Sherman's work was shaped by Andy Warhol.

10.4324/9781003106685-18

- Tina Modotti's work was changed by Edward Weston.
- Richard Tuschman's photos were affected by Edward Hopper.
- Man Ray – Pablo Picasso, Wassily Kandinsky, and Marcel Duchamp.
- David LaChapelle was guided by Caravaggio's paintings.
- Gemmy Woud-Binnendijk admired Rembrandt.
- Gertrude Fehr respected Man Ray.
- Bettina Rheims revered Diane Arbus and Helmut Newton.
- Pieter Hugo prized the work of David Goldblatt and Boris Mikhailov.

This list could go on. The lesson to be learned here is that something or someone influences most every successful photographer's creative practice. There are two myths that are popular among students of photography: "I don't like to look at other people's artwork because I don't want to copy them" and "My work will be more original if I don't look at other artist's work." This way of thinking simply isn't true. This isn't how your memory works. Your brain can't look at a photo and then, consciously or unconsciously, produce an exact copy. If it did, your brain would remember everything you study for your classes and you'd get 100 percent on all your exams! These myths are perpetuated mainly out of laziness.

When you look at artwork that attracts you, your neurons go straight to work decoding visual stimuli so it can understand what it's looking at. It does this by translating visual imagery into visual language, then into verbal language. Using these languages, the brain will store impressions as memories (remember the greenhouses in Chapter 14?) that are made of those images' meaningful information.

When you look at artworks that excite you, you are observing examples of ingenious creative solutions. They are examples of complex compositional and artistic problems that other people solved. Studying masterful artworks provides experiences that you can use to develop your own creative abilities.

By internalizing the ways these artists solved problems, the art can serve as a resource for your future image-making, your use of visual language, and your skills for artistic problem-solving. In a way, others' art helps you to better understand your own visual language. These historical and contemporary artworks you seek out and visually consume are like rocket fuel for your creativity. This is what great art does in your brain!

Pablo Picasso once said, "Good artists copy, great artists steal." In this case, your brain is recording impressions of great artworks, decoding them, storing them in its neural network as data, then accessing those memories when needed. Again, don't worry about unconsciously or accidentally stealing someone else's images. Your brain won't provide enough detailed information to cause you to duplicate someone else's photographs. Through the creative process, these memories become a mashup of ideas. Original ideas then arise. Creative inspirations are "Frankensteined" together from lots of different memory impressions. Or, as Kirby Ferguson puts it, "The most dramatic results can happen when ideas are combined. By connecting ideas together, creative leaps can be made, producing some of history's biggest breakthroughs."[84]

It's possible that creative leaps can be made by emulating some of the ingenious qualities of your favorite artists. In other words, you can model your work on, or pay homage to, someone else's work as a learning exercise. Seek out the connections that you have with those artworks and emulate their subject matter or style with the intention of seeing where it leads in the development of your own work. This exercise will definitely take you somewhere. Think of emulation as a kind of apprenticeship with those photographers whose work you find inspiring, meaningful, and emotionally moving. Look at the work of accomplished artists and trust that it has the potential to teach you something about the importance and direction of your own work.

Another lesser-known myth comes from the idea that "I don't want to look at great art, because it reminds me that I will never be able to do anything like that." This is like saying that you don't want to eat amazing, gourmet food because you will never be able to cook it! Don't worry about making photos as good or as creative as Sherrie Levine or Tim Walker. Keep moving forward on your path one step at a time. Consume valuable visual impressions, so your brain can digest this raw material as the essential nutrients needed for creative nourishment. Your superpower will become stronger, and your abilities will grow!

Be curious about what kind of art exists in your areas of interest. It's important that you look at lots of photographs that express a wide range of emotions, ideas, concepts, and conclusions. Try to awaken that sense of curiosity and even look at photographs you don't particularly connect with. Ask yourself questions like, "What is it about Chuck Close's photos that got them hanging on the walls of the Museum of Modern Art?" "Why is Nick Ut's photography considered to be significant?" "What is Roger Ballen thinking and experiencing when he makes his dark, psychological portraits?" "Who proclaimed the photos by the Photo-Secessionists to be so influential as to change the photography world from that point forward?" When looking at Robert Mapplethorpe's photos, ask: "What kind of reactions did the culture and society of that time have for these photographs?"

The more questions you ask, the more possible it becomes to imagine seeing through that photographer's eyes. Also, the more accessible those memories will be for you during future brainstorming and image-making. Your active curiosity about artists' works will improve your creative abilities and lead you toward finding more pieces in the big-picture puzzle of your unique photographic style. It will allow you to solve problems in new ways by using what you have learned over time. Let great art guide you toward new ways of thinking about unfamiliar perspectives, while adding more fuel to your creative fire.

Part 5
Learn

19

How to Ace Assignments

Be PREPARED

If you want to excel with your assignments, then this chapter will guide you through a step-by-step process that can lead you to success. Over the course of the semester, you will complete a series of projects, each building on the skills and knowledge you learned from previous assignments. It's a method called *scaffolded* learning. Your professors put a lot of thought into designing coursework that is scaffolded and engaging. They come up with lessons that are technically and intellectually challenging, targeted to your learning level.

Your instructors know that the best way to learn something is by putting that learning to use. For example, to effectively understand how to use your camera, you start by watching a video or receiving instruction that gives you a basic conceptual understanding. Then you have to apply that new knowledge by picking up a camera and making photos. You look at examples of successful photos, but only by experimenting with the settings will you know with certainty the difference between what your photo will look like by setting your shutter speed on 1/8, as opposed to 1/1000 second.

Trial and error is a powerful experiential learning method, because it gives you immediate feedback. You can see a direct correlation between the shutter-speed settings and how that affects the appearance of the subject on your viewscreen. Each experiment you do produces evidence of your learning. That is how you learn. As Confucius once said, "Tell me, and I will forget. Show me, and I will remember. Involve me, and I will understand forever."

Once you receive an assignment, you start thinking about what you need to do to fulfill the requirements in the allotted time. Your goal as a student

DOI: 10.4324/9781003106685-19

photographer is to take the parameters of the assignment and make images that demonstrate a unique, creative approach to the subject matter. Your images should also express your vision, skills, and abilities. The photos should be compelling, inviting the observer to look and want to spend a few moments to explore and discover. Using subject matter, composition, light, and shadow shows viewers how you are able to artfully elevate the importance of the subject matter. Provide them with something more than a photograph. Give them a meaningful viewing experience based on the unique way you perceived the scene.

Assignments can be better understood by breaking them down into three stages: *pre-production*, *production*, and *post-production*. Each stage presents you with a series of choices that prepare you for success in the next stage. The attention you give to the details of each stage pays off by reducing the time, energy, and mental focus that will be needed in subsequent steps in the process.

PRE-PRODUCTION

The whole activity starts when your instructor assigns the project, and that's when the *pre-production* stage begins. The assignment description should provide a topic and explanation for the goals you are supposed to achieve. Begin by reading the information from beginning to end. Listen to what your instructor says about the project. Take notes. If you don't understand something, ask for clarification. Highlight all instructional details about the parameters of the assignment. Here is a list of seven crucial points that you need to know so you are prepared for the pre-production success.

1. A detailed description of the assignment topic or theme and an explanation of what's expected of you.
2. Objectives, learning objectives, or outcomes. This information tells you what you are supposed to learn as a result of the assignment. The objectives could be about learning facts, gaining knowledge that comes from direct experience, engaging important practices that will prepare you for future learning, opportunities for critical or analytical thinking, situations that persuade you to reflect on concepts, or the assignment may help you acquire metacognitive knowledge (helps you think about what you think).
3. Procedures. Some assignments come with specific technical requirements you need to successfully fulfill to meet the project goals. For example, you may be required to use a digital camera to produce both RAW and jpg files. Other technical requisites may ask you to use specific lighting, subject matter, or particular exposure settings.
4. Tips and examples. These are optional with assignment instructions, but always appreciated! When they are provided, they can offer insight

into the assignment and/or help you avoid common pitfalls and obstacles throughout the production stages. Good examples can become creative fuel and also spark ideas!

5. The result. You need to know how many photos to produce, how many image files you should turn in, and which format the files/images have to be in (RAW files, jpg files, prints, or a book). You also need to know if images are supposed to be posted to a website, uploaded to a shared folder, or sent to a classroom site in a Course Management System.
6. Rubric. A rubric explains how you will be graded. It establishes a direct relationship between what you need to do and the criteria by which it will be graded. The rubric tells you which aspects of the assignment will serve as evidence that you met the learning objectives. For pre-production, the rubric helps you know where to focus your attention and energy when planning how to approach the assignment.
7. Timetable. Assignments come with a due date. Once you know when the project has to be turned in, and you understand all the parameters, it's time to get organized. You can begin pre-production planning by taking to heart the saying, "Failure to plan is planning to fail." Start a dialogue with your instructor to learn about their expectations for a finished product. Your instructor needs to see that your final photos are high quality and a good example of what they wants you to learn. Even though you have detailed guidelines and objectives, there is usually a lot of freedom to photograph the subject matter of your choice, along with how you would like to photograph it. Your instructor will probably encourage you to challenge yourself by taking a creative approach that entails some creative risk.

When you have an idea for a project, present it to your instructor and your CSN to get their opinions and advice. Apply any usable feedback, especially from your instructor. Getting advice is an important part of the pre-production stage of your assignment. Good advice and planning will help you be PREPARED (Plan, Research, Envision, Place, Assistance, Rembrandt, Equipment, and Deadline).

Plan

Your brain has a limited capacity for focused attention and processing. To reserve the highest processing capacity possible during your photo session, plan ahead. Anticipate potential problems before they arise, and solve as many of them as you can before you pick up a camera. Planning helps you feel prepared, because you know what to expect in the process. Planning supports your goal to meet the completion deadline. Knowing that some of the problems have been resolved ahead of time can lessen feelings of anxiety, help you feel more confident, and allow you to hold your attention on the creative problems that arise during production. Consider important questions like:

- Who is your audience?
- What is your concept or theme for your assignment?
- Which format will you use: square, 35mm, panorama, or other?
- Will you need models, locations, equipment, or props? And, if so, how will you get them?
- What could go wrong? And, if it does, how can you get through these obstacles?

Research

Go online and look at examples of how other photographers approached the same assignment or subject matter. See if anyone made images like the kind you envision for your own photos. Find examples of inspiring successes and use what you learn as inspiration. Inspiration gets you excited! Start a Pinterest board of the artworks you find most exciting. With you as the curator, think of this board as the art exhibition you would most like to see. It should contain all of your favorite pieces (photo, painting, printmaking, etc.). When you need an inspirational boost, go back and look at your art collection.

Envision

Envision or pre-visualize the photos you want as an end product. If you can pre-visualize your final photos, you can use backward planning to figure out how to get what you want. Wildlife photographer Melissa Groo advises,

> it really helps to have a desired image in your mind and then work backward from that, taking into account each element that's an integral piece of the whole. Rough drafts are often needed and failed attempts are to be expected. But if you have a vision and are methodical in your approach to achieve that vision, I really believe you will meet with success.[1]

At the same time be open to serendipity, happenstance, and fortuitousness! When unexpected surprises pop up, photographic magic can happen! Pursue your vision, while at the same time not letting expectations or a sense of perfectionism limit your ideas about what a successful photo has to look like.

Place

Is your photo session going to be in a studio or on-location? If it's at a location, where? Have you found the prospective location? "As you set out to evaluate locations, you'll likely face countless possibilities: natural areas, historic sites, distinctive buildings, urban landscapes and waterfront settings, to name a few."[2] Figure out the best time of day for your location and estimate how long you expect to be there. Scout locations for lighting information and accessibility, so you can be better prepared. This is just one of the many details you need to plan for to increase your chances for a successful photo shoot.

Assistance

Do you need help to successfully achieve your technical and conceptual goals? Assemble and use your PLN and CSN. You may also need people to assist you or serve as models. If so, set a date and time and get everyone's contact information. If others are assisting you at the photo shoot, be prepared, so they can get in and get out quickly. Because everyone's time is valuable, volunteers get annoyed and resentful when they show up on time and the photographer isn't ready. The longer they have to wait, the less likely your assistants will help out next time.

Rembrandt

Think about how Rembrandt (master of light and shadow) would successfully light your subject. WWRD? ("What would Rembrandt do?") Consider lighting (quality, direction, intensity, and color). Rembrandt used light to create drama, and so can you. Also, from Rembrandt's perspective, challenge yourself to take some creative risks and break some new ground in your photo practice by experimenting with light. Pre-visualize your photos and ask, "WWRD?"

Equipment

Make a list of everything you will need for your photo sessions (see equipment check-off sheet on www.photostudent.net > Resources > Appendix). Most importantly, consider the camera you will use. There is no "best" camera for all situations. Each kind of camera produces images with their own special visual qualities and file sizes. It's important to consider whether or not the visual qualities of the camera you choose will support the theme of your photos. Ultimately, the kind of camera you choose is second in importance to what you can do with that camera!

Deadline

The world runs on deadlines, and part of your academic experience is designed to help you establish a habit of meeting deadlines. You practice daily deadlines when you get to class on time. Photo assignments have deadlines in the form of due dates. Make a schedule with due dates for everything you need to finish during pre-production, production, and post-production. Figure out how you will use your time and energy management to be PREPARED to meet your goals when transitioning from pre-production to production.

PRODUCTION

Now that you have some understanding of pre-production, it's time to learn about the *production* phase. This second stage is the time you spend using the camera, composing the subject and making photographs. Photographer Adrian Vila believes that taking the photo is the least important part of photography.[3] If you think about how much time and energy you devote to the pre- and post-production stages in relation to the fraction of a second it takes to capture the image, his theory starts to make sense. Yet, for most photographers the significance of making the images during production can't be stressed enough. It is the moment when you get to feel the first rush of photographic pleasure!

If you were thorough during the pre-production phase, you can thank your past self for helping you out. Attention to detail during pre-production allows you to focus all of your energy on getting great photographs. You don't have to worry about what you want to photograph or use up mental bandwidth trying to remember if you have everything you need. You can let go of the stress that comes with being unprepared – because you are prepared! You have everything you need in your bags, cases, notes, and checklists. You can rely on those checklists to help you feel focused and confident that you are ready to begin. That being said, the truth is that sometimes things don't go exactly as planned. There are always plenty of opportunities for creative problem-solving. Planning, though, minimizes many of the unfavorable surprises during production. Still, unexpected things do pop up, just to keep your photo session exciting.

During production, take on the role of a director, just like the director of a movie! You're in charge of translating the subject matter into your visionary, visual expression, your story. You bring your way of seeing the world to the image-making process by figuring out how to capture that vision in a photographic frame. A director is never passive, but proactive. Explore many angles, use a variety of lens focal lengths, perspectives (shoot from eye level, above eye level, and below eye level), and explore all the photographic possibilities. Zoom with your feet (walk closer and farther away to change your vantage point). Move around. Look up and down, look behind you for unexpected vantage points. Carry out all your plans from pre-production, but then capture something completely different, and as compelling, as your pre-visualization! Remember: intention with spontaneity.

Everything in your composition should contribute to your story. Your photos may speak about beauty, the human condition, the decisive moment, urban decay, or your family. Whatever the subject matter, use all the elements of the composition to support your story. Eliminate elements that don't contribute, that distract or confuse your viewers or take their attention away from your message, your vision.

As a final production tip, try to capture the scene in a way that it is as close to your vision as possible. In other words, don't get in the habit of making photos with the intention of fixing them in post-production. Fix the photos now so you will spend less time in post-production editing. Get in the habit of taking the extra time to fix the lighting, wait for the clouds to be in the right place, remove the visual distractions, set up that tripod if needed, or dig out that other lens from your bag – the one that produces great bokeh (the painterly quality of out-of-focus areas of an image). That kind of attention to detail will prepare you for success in post-production. It will make you happier in the end. As the saying goes, "Pre-touch instead of retouch." Get it right when you capture the image, so you don't have to fix it in post-production.

POST-PRODUCTION

You made it to the final phase of your assignment! You have captured your images and it's time for post-production editing and file management. With editing, you have the opportunity to finish your photos, to prepare them for presentation, and to bring them more in line with your vision. In a perfect world, you use your time in post-production to enhance and finish your photos, not fix them.

Establish an efficient post-production workflow (your preferred sequence of steps from downloading and organizing files to the final product). Workflow is important, because it's a habitual routine that will end up saving you a lot of time. Post-production workflow usually includes processing files, organizing, global edits like cropping out distractions along the edges of the frame, exposure adjustments, contrast to increase visual impact, resizing, and file conversion for output. After global editing, you can zoom in to focus on the details with local edits, like removing spots or cloning.

Finally, in the last step of editing you will sharpen your images before preparing your files, based on the specifications of the assignment. You will upload files or submit prints for critique and so your instructor can offer feedback. Make sure to back up all your files on a separate computer, online, or an external hard drive (never store or work on files from a portable USB flash drive!). You will likely learn a more detailed post-production workflow process from your instructor, based on the technology used in your program. Also, there are a wide variety of books and tutorials online that will show you how to use both Adobe Lightroom and Adobe Photoshop – important tools that enhance your images in post-production.

20

Be a RISK Taker

The practice of making photos deliberately and intentionally can be broken down into two parts. First, turn on your brain before you turn on your camera. When you're out taking photos, follow your immediate impulse to get that shot. After that, pause for a moment. Deliberately observe by focusing your attention on the subject matter. Ansel Adams said,

> In my mind's eye, I visualize how a particular … sight and feeling will appear on a print. If it excites me, there is a good chance it will make a good photograph. It is an intuitive sense, an ability that comes from a lot of practice.[88]

Everything you see can be interesting if you look closely enough. When you take notice, it awakens a sense of curiosity. It helps you recognize visual aspects of the subject that are meaningful, interesting, expressive, exciting, fascinating, thought-provoking, and that attract your eye.

You don't have to think about what you see – just take it all in, and when that feeling comes up, respond with your camera. By shifting attention away from thinking and your senses, your brain will allocate more processing power to your field of vision. Transferring your attention in this way makes your sense of sight hypersensitive, hyperreceptive, and hyperperceptive.

For instance, when you put all of your attention on what your eyes see, you can achieve a state that some photographers call *being in the zone*. This basically means that you may not be aware of everything that's happening around you,

10.4324/9781003106685-20

like sounds, smells, and sensations from the environment. You enter a state of visual sensitivity where you perceive details and qualities you otherwise don't notice when you glance at a scene as you normally would.

The practice is to look long enough, deeply enough, that you are open to intuitively feel when an impulse comes up, to capture that magical quality you see as a scene. Your photos will communicate something about what you discovered during your observation, whether it's something important or completely unremarkable and ordinary. Be mindful that, if you don't recognize something special in the scene you are photographing, then it's likely your audience won't, either. It's your choice. You can simply show someone what was in front of your camera or you can elevate the subject matter by showing the viewer the special way you see the subject. This decision depends largely on your level of perceptual ability, and your intention to photograph, combined with your level of photographic skill.

Insights you gain during the first step of deliberate practice will largely determine the success of your photograph in the second step: composing and capturing the photo. By practicing with intention, you counteract the brain's tendency to place judgments on what you see while willfully overlooking much of what is in its field of view. Seeing, framing, and composing changes the habit of superficially scanning the world, while your perception remains on autopilot. The more photos you can make in a deliberate way, the more you will grow in skill and ability toward becoming a creative, masterful photographer.

When faced with any creative decision, your brain tends to choose the path that's most familiar and comfortable. Deliberate photography practice establishes a new habit of exploring and observing your subject from multiple, informed perspectives. As Scott Kelby recommends, "work the scene."[89] Kelby recommends you look up, look down, turn around, and look behind you. Crouch down and get on the ground to experience the worm's-eye view. Climb up on something to get a higher vantage point. You can't know what the best angle is until you see what each of the angles reveal. Your willingness to slow down and observe, work the scene, and take some creative risks can expose visual treasures that most people miss! Transitioning out of old habits and into new habits feels like a risk, but it's a risk worth taking.

Certainty, comfort, safety, conformity, and stability – these are things everyone wants so they don't feel uncomfortable. If you only act out of comfort and caution, you will never awaken the full capacity of your creative energy. Instead, try to make risk-taking a habitual part of your photography practice. To do so requires your willingness to move outside your comfort zone, to find ways to overcome your resistance to seeing the world in new ways. Be willing to challenge your mindset, to do the things you've decided you won't do, even if it helps to evolve your photography practice. Just to be clear: this doesn't mean taking risks that challenge your *safety zone*. Your practice shouldn't ever put you in danger! Instead, confront the obstacles that are holding you back. They are thoughts like:

1. I won't go out when it's raining, snowing, dark, etc.
2. I won't travel anywhere I've never been.
3. I won't ask people for help.
4. I won't leave my couch.
5. I won't cut into my Netflix time.
6. I won't get my gear together, because I don't know what I want to take pictures of.
7. I won't wake up early (or stay up really late).
8. I won't make people think I'm weird.
9. I won't be inconvenienced.
10. I won't try it, because it makes me uncomfortable.
11. I won't ______________________________ [add your own reason].

Dare yourself to experiment with new ideas. Become curious. Embrace the motto of What if ...?" For instance, *what if* your composition made a subject look abstract? *What if* you physically fabricated your entire photographic subject? What would happen if you photographed something you have an aversion to, like spiders, or something from a very high vantage point? What would it look like if you got up at 5:00 a.m. to capture a subject in the light of the sunrise? From another perspective, what if you could find a nonprofit organization and volunteer your photographic services for a couple of hours, or a day? During that volunteer time, make images of whatever they would like you to photograph. Then, give them copies of all the files, no strings attached. For some people, this would be outside their comfort zone.

Creative risk doesn't mean becoming a war correspondent who puts their life in danger on a daily basis, like photographers Matthew Brady or James Nachtwey. It is more about overcoming mental resistance to try something that's new to you, something unfamiliar. Think of it as being curious and not letting your self-doubt and fear of failure prevent you from taking advantage of opportunities to become a more experienced photographer. Maybe you are afraid people won't like your photos, or they might not like you. Dancer Twyla Tharp says in her book *The Creative Habit: Learn it and Use it for Life* that her biggest fears, which prevent her from taking creative risks, are:

1. People will laugh at me.
2. Someone has done it before.
3. I have nothing to say.
4. I will upset someone I love.
5. Once executed, the idea will never be as good as it is in my mind.[90]

Tharp goes on to say that "These are mighty demons." Make it your goal to ignore the negative voices in your head, but instead act on imaginative ideas. Don't worry about who will see the photos or what people may think. You have total control over *who, when,* and *if* anyone sees the photos. You could decide to not show them to anyone at all. Again, you have total control over who sees your photos.

Consider taking creative risks as a personal challenge. The experiment can't fail! You'll either end up with interesting photos or you'll succeed because your courage provided you with valuable experience. The experience could end up being more important than the images you get. And maybe that experience is a necessary step toward new creative ideas.

Here is a creative risk assignment based on experience and learning. Go out on a photo walk and make 100 photos. When you are finished, write down 10 things you learned from the experience. Then, go against the rules of your photographic practice and delete all the files. Let the photos remain only in your brain's memory. This is an experiment. But there is much to be learned from trying it. Or, in the words of Neil Gaiman, "If you dare nothing, then when the day is over, nothing is all you will have gained."[91]

Selling your photo service to clients can also feel like a risk. First, learn everything you can about what your customer needs. Second, give them a quote for how much it will cost, hoping that everything will go right and you will make some money. If they hire you, strive to meet your client's expectations. It's stressful at first, because you know that people are depending on you to deliver high-quality photos, usually on a tight deadline. You are expected to be professional in your appearance and with your actions. For a student, this can be a very new experience. Taking on a client for the first time is a nerve-racking, yet rewarding risk. You will succeed or fail. If you fail, you'll learn the hard way. Next time, you won't forget what to do and what not to do.

Here are three other cases to consider for increasing your risk factor:

1. The first time you show or exhibit new work can be stressful. If you need some encouragement to take the first step toward showing your photos, ask your instructor for feedback and support for your ideas. You could also ask friends for some confidence-building support. Also take advantage of your CSN and PLN.
2. Let's say you get a good idea for photos, but it's something you're nervous about pursuing. Creative risks lead you into unknown, unfamiliar territory and it's a little scary, especially if you have an idea that's truly worth pursuing. Do some research and see if any other photographers have produced images from similar ideas. If so, take what they started to the next level. Get help if you need it. Bounce some ideas back and forth with your CSN and PLN communities.
3. Many photographs could be improved by simply moving closer to the subject. For some photographers, this feels uncomfortable. It seems especially risky when photographing people, even though doing so can add an extra emotional dimension to the portrait. Rick Sammon points out that the closer you are to the subject, the more intimate the photo will feel.[92] Beginning photographers feel uneasy about moving in, yet doing so is a low-stakes risk that can yield visual impact for the viewer.

Landscape photographer Erin Babnik offers some advice.

> When a photograph departs from some kind of norm, a portion of your audience may not "get" it. Accept that familiarity is appealing to most people, and that not everyone who typically enjoys your photographs will cheer you on enthusiastically down whatever trail you may blaze. Even if your experiments do not result in immediate encouragement, there could be momentum building, and if that is the case, then you will only ever realize it if you stay the course. Regardless, doing something unconventional is gutsy, and that point in itself should provide a certain degree of satisfaction and motivation. Knowing that you are being true to yourself is a source of real power that can continue to propel you forward.[93]

Try to push past fear and anxiety, so you can learn from the lessons that come from breaking new ground.

RISK

The above mnemonic summarizes what it means to take risks as part of your deliberate photography practice. When you are in a situation where you are faced with a choice either to take the easy, comfortable path or the path that steers you out of your comfort zone, remember: Resolve, Imagination, Surprise, and Knowledge.

- *Resolve*. Resolve to overcome your fear of failure or whatever prevents you from taking creative risks! Enjoy the rewards when the risk pays off.
- *Imagination*. Einstein said that "imagination is more important than knowledge. For knowledge is limited, whereas imagination embraces the entire world, stimulating progress, giving birth to evolution." Use your imagination to visualize the creative photos that a great idea and risk can yield.
- *Surprise*. Surprise yourself by doing something that goes beyond your self-imposed limitations! Be open to whatever happens.
- *Knowledge*. Every experiment provides important information that you can use in future photo sessions. If your risk doesn't pay off, learn everything you can from the failure and think of it as an opportunity to learn what didn't work. Gaining knowledge is what helps you grow in skill and ability.

21

Motivation Leads to Productivity

The secret to what motivates any of us is pretty simple: we want to do things we enjoy, that bring us pleasure. When an activity gives you pleasure, it activates the reward centers in your brain, it makes you happy, and you feel motivated to continue doing it. For instance, if you are looking through your viewfinder and you see something that thrills you, you aim the camera and push the shutter release. Something motivated you to take the shot and, as a result, you received a little reward, a bit of pleasure. This is one example, among many, for how motivation works to provide energy for your photography practice. This chapter explores several kinds of motivators that you can use for the benefit of your photo studies and practice.

If you know what motivates and inspires you, it can help you tap into the energy you need to take actions that can help you achieve your goals. It's not enough to have great ideas. You have to be able to perform, to produce, to focus the energy that will make those ideas real. Motivation is an impulse, an energy that compels you do to something, even if you don't feel like doing it. You just have to learn how to harness the energy so you can use it to its full potential!

By knowing what motivates you, you can create the circumstances you need to feel inspired, to set goals and get things done. Author Maria Konnikova says that "Students who are motivated perform better … motivation predicts higher academic performance … better employment outcomes … and are more likely to be successful in any number of endeavors, from art to science."[94]

Let's say you're motivated by good grades and you feel driven to get a 4.0 in your class. Understanding that about yourself can cause you to work closely with

10.4324/9781003106685-21

your professor, follow the instructions on the syllabus, and pay attention to how your finished assignment photos line up with the expected outcomes on the rubrics. This is an example of extrinsic motivation, or something that compels you to take action and want to excel because there is an expectation of reward, recognition, praise from others, the promise of a future job, or to achieve some kind of status.

Extrinsic motivation energizes you to make photos with the hope that people will like them, maybe even enough to buy them! Or to hope your images will get you lots of "likes" on Facebook and Instagram. That praise and recognition drives you to focus on your photography and maybe even to be productive. If it matters to you that your professors, peers, and others think highly of your work and your level of performance, then these are the extrinsic forces that can help you turn your attention toward your work.

Don't try to reason out why you feel motivated by these factors, because the reasons probably aren't rational or logical. Whatever they are, try to accept them. Motivations aren't inherently good or bad. They are characteristics that everyone has. Think of them as tools your brain provides as fuel to power you on the path toward learning and achievement.

Other motivators, like procrastination, could put you in a tough spot. An example of this might be feeling motivated to go on a photography walk so you can put off, or procrastinate, doing your Biology homework. In other words, avoiding something you don't want to do can be a tremendous motivator! If you think the outcome will be rewarding, you may make sacrifices to do what you *want* to do instead of doing what you are *supposed* to do – especially if you tend to procrastinate.

The other kind of driving force is intrinsic motivation. For example, making photos can provide its own rewards in the form of enjoyment and a sense of gratification. You might be a talented photographer who feels pleasure from exercising your sense of curiosity or by being attracted to a creative challenge or the sense of adventure that photography can provide. You could be motivated to pick up your camera and go treasure hunting, looking for images because you enjoy the sense of discovery while using your artistic ability to capture photos. Because the practice of photography can help build your confidence, it can cause you to feel self-satisfied in your abilities.

If you are a photographer who didn't start out with a natural talent for image-making, you may be motivated to improve your skills. You can get excited by the challenge of practicing in order gradually to become a better photographer. Maybe the source of your motivation is to improve and excel. You can feel a sense of pride in your hard work and a sense of accomplishment with your photos. These are all intrinsic motivators, where rewards come from within.

Psychologist Abraham Maslow said that the highest stages of personal motivation are the need for "Esteem: prestige and feeling of accomplishment" and "Self-actualization: achieving one's full potential, including creative activities."[95] Maslow believed that these needs are integral behaviors within every person's psychological makeup. They are needs that can be understood as common intrinsic motivators among all people. Identify your own intrinsic motivators, but don't be surprised if you feel connected to a mix of both intrinsic and extrinsic ones.

Daniel Pink, author of *Drive: The Surprising Truth About What Motivates Us*, says there are three primary intrinsic motivators: autonomy, mastery, and purpose.[96] *Autonomy*, in this case, could be understood as the freedom to photograph what you want, when you want, and how you want. You and your camera are free to do whatever you like. You are motivated to discover and develop your own style without being censored or restricted.

When Daniel Pink talks about *mastery*, he's talking about being motivated to achieve a high degree of competence doing something you feel is important and meaningful to you. You may be driven to improve constantly, and to climb up through the levels of skill and ability toward mastery. With this category, it's understood that you are inherently motivated to become an expert photographer.

If you feel that your photography practice is meaningful in a way that provides a sense of *purpose*, it can motivate you to practice your photography. You may be compelled to make photos for a higher purpose, such as to help others. For example, purpose can motivate you to create images that can affect positive change in social justice, racial equality, or climate change awareness.

Being aware of what motivates you can lead you toward confidence in the projects you choose to do as a photographer. If you can identify what motivates you to make photos, you can use that energy to make your way up the levels toward mastery: "One of the great benefits of knowing your motivations is that knowledge can help you find opportunities where you're both likely to succeed and be deeply fulfilled."[97] You can also use that insight to take more responsibility for your learning experience and more pleasure in your accomplishments. As a warning, don't put yourself in a box. As you grow and evolve in your photography practice, your primary motivations may change. Be open to allowing the sources of your motivation to change over time and take advantage of whatever inspirations may come.

Here are six additional topics that may motivate you to pursue your photography practice actively:

1. *Understanding.* You will naturally be more excited to make photos when you understand how meaningful this creative activity is in the way it relates to your interests, your passions, and your life.
2. *Negative consequences.* The desire to avert negative consequences, like getting a poor grade or having to pay a fine motivates lots of students to perform. Academic grading systems rely on the threat of negative consequences to persuade students to meet deadlines and try to excel in their studies. Some students work hard because they don't want to feel like they have let down their classmates, instructors, or parents. They feel accountable to themselves and others so they do what it takes to avoid negative consequences.

3. *Curiosity*. Try to nurture this motivation as much as you can. *Needing to know* is a fundamental motivator for human beings. It is a motivator that has, over the course of history, caused civilizations to evolve and has produced many great artworks and inventions. It is a creative force that can be destroyed by fear. Pema Chodron reminds us all to "Let your curiosity be greater than your fear."[98] Allow your curiosity to take you to places you have never been, experience things you have never encountered, and fill your mind with fascinating material that will feed your imagination!
4. *Daily life experiences*. You can even draw motivational energy from the emotional rollercoaster of happy, sad, fun, and boring daily events in your life. You could choose to use photography as a habitual response to whatever random circumstances are affecting you right now. For example, if you feel withdrawn or frustrated, express your emotional/psychological state by making images that incorporate those feelings. If your pet dies, let that tragedy motivate you to make some photos that honor the life of your pet. If you fall in love, express what that feels like by using your images. You've heard of the old saying "Use your words." In this case, "Use your pictures"!

   If you feel proud of yourself because you just won an award or just met someone you *really* like, find a way to incorporate those feelings into your photos. The point is that you can choose to be motivated by your daily experiences. Someone once said that you can't control what happens to you in life, but you can control how you respond. *Choose* to be motivated by your feelings about life events and use that energy to respond like a photographer.
5. *Deadlines*. Having to work under a deadline is very common in both academia and as part of a professional life after graduation. Your formal education is designed to make deadlines a common part of your workflow. Your instructors hope you will learn how to use intrinsic and extrinsic motivators to manage your time in a way that assures you will be motivated to meet your assignment deadlines.
6. *Goals*. Some people are goal oriented and feel motivated by their sense of determination and commitment to reach their objectives. For example, here are the three top goals, rated by level of importance, that motivate lots of photographers:
   i. Publish a book of personal work.
   ii. Receive wide-ranging recognition.
   iii. Make enough money with photography to have a comfortable living.

Coaches are experts at motivating others to excel beyond their self-imposed limitations. An effective instructor can be the same thing for students, especially the ones that have a plan for reaching personal goals. If you are motivated to pursue important individual, creative goals, then you may find this quote from Hyperfit USA to be inspiring. It's designed to fire-up their members, and to get them committed, to motivate them to reach the peak of their personal potential:

People often see the champion astride the podium receiving awards and praise. What people do not see are the heart-wrenching struggles it took to get there.

People often see the fruit of the tree, but never the struggle the tree had going from the seed to the mature tree. Success comes from commitment.

Commitment means making something you want a priority and being determined to achieve it. It means doing the same work whether someone is watching or not. It means passing up some of those fun things "other" people do since you are committed to your goal. It means measuring and valuing the things you have in your life in terms of how much they support or hinder your commitment to your goal.

Commitment means having the strength to discard that which does not help you get what you want. Commitment means seeking people and ideas that foster your goal.

The prize of commitment is not the podium, but the step-by-step process of getting there. The journey of commitment and its value comes from reshaping yourself into something closer to your potential. It has been theorized that self-actualization is the peak of individual accomplishment.

Let's find out.[99]

Motivation provides the dynamic energy needed to help you focus on taking action. It's also the energy that can help you overcome obstacles and solve problems that can prevent you from reaching your goals. To help you know more about your own motivations, here are some statements that you may identify with. Take a look and note which of these lines describe something that motivates you to stand, pick up your camera, and do what needs to be done to make some photos.

- Someone I admire was/is passionate about photography and they inspire me.
- I want to work for a photography-based business (National Geographic, Aperture, etc.).
- When making photos, I escape reality for a while.
- I thrive on the emotional response I get from the people I photograph.
- I thrive on the emotional response I get from the people who view my photos.
- I love to share my experiences with others.
- Doing something creative energizes me.
- Making photos helps relieve my stress and anxiety.
- I'm motivated by the desire/need to make things.
- I love the extra support it gives financially.
- I'm curious about seeing what things look like in photos.
- I want to express my thoughts and ideas about things that interest me.
- I like to document my experiences as a visual journal.
- I want to document the lives of my friends, siblings, or someone else.

- The work of amazing photographers and/or artists inspires me.
- I hope to relive the moment when I get a shot I love.
- Photography is part of my love of the outdoors.
- It's fun visiting galleries or museums and feeling inspired.
- I enjoy critiquing other people's portfolios.
- It motivates me when I explore the photography section of my library.
- I like to learn by watching photo tutorials or videos on photography.
- TED talks on photography or photographers (or any TED Talks) energize me.
- I get fired-up by taking a photo workshop or class during summer break.
- I make photos because it gives me a feeling of belonging.
- I'm motivated to make photos because it's my creative outlet (I can't draw, paint, or write stories).
- It feels good when others tell me how much they like my photos.
- I enjoy opening Instagram and seeing how many people "liked" my photos.
- When I go to a photo conference, it gets me fired up to make new work!

Make a list of 10 more things that motivate you to make photographs. Feel free to include any from the above list, but be honest with yourself. Then, arrange the 10 items with the strongest as number 1, and so on down to number 10. Now you have 10 points of self-knowledge that you can take advantage of to rouse energy for your photography practice.

One of the most reliable motivators for photographers is *anticipation*. If you understand the feeling of motivation as an energy that advances your photo practice, then consider how a sense of anticipation can be a source of ongoing energetic support. If you were a superhero, anticipation would be a major source of energy for your superpower. There are at least two times when the motivating energy of anticipation comes into play during your photo practice: while you have a camera in your hand, you are looking through the viewfinder, and you are taking photos: and during post-production editing.

As you look through your camera, the energy of anticipation emerges from a kind of excitement about the possibility that your next photo could truly be something exciting. The moment is full of potential for the chance of taking a photo that meets or exceeds your expectations. It's the pure potential of looking forward to what could happen between you, your camera, and the subject every time you look through the lens. The energy puts you in a state of expectation, waiting to see what the next photo will look like. It's like feeling eager to know the end of a story, with the plot twist at the last moment when you push the shutter release.

Imagine having your senses on high alert so you can capture the action of your subject at the perfect time. Henri Cartier-Bresson was able to utilize anticipation so he could "capture this fleeting, quintessential, and holistic instant in the flow of life."[100] Sports photographers become experts at riding the energetic wave of anticipation so they can see ahead of the action. As coach Wayne

Gretzky told his hockey players, "Skate to where the puck is going, not where it has been." A masterful sports photographer needs to anticipate not only when to make the photograph, but also where to aim the lens, where everything *is going to happen*. The energy behind making photos is the anticipation that motivates photographers to imagine how the shot will look before they capture the image.

Embracing anticipation activates the primal, animalistic parts of the brain, the fight-or-flight response that keeps your photographer's brain alert and on edge, prepared for whatever surprises come up. And whatever happens you will be ready, like a reflex action to push the shutter release!

The post-production phase of your workflow offers much the same kind of feeling/energy of anticipation as when you edit photos. The energy compels you to go through the steps of editing so you can *make real* your pre-visualized image as a real end product. Only by reaching the finished image can you know for sure if the photo you made meets your expectations and is worthy of replacing the weakest image in your portfolio. If it is, then you get to feel elated (a feeling that you anticipate)! Whether or not it is worthy, you will likely feel motivated to pick up your camera again so you can try again to achieve that goal. Doing so may come with an emotional reward!

Finally, if you need a quick motivational boost, read some of the quotes provided in Chapters 29 and 30. These short pieces of advice can inspire you and move you to action. There are quotes on topics such as your photography practice, assignments, critique, your career, photography tools, and mentors. Great quotes like these offer new perspectives on subjects that are important to you, causing you to deepen your curiosity and desire to learn. They can encourage you to be productive, to take a chance and break new ground with your creativity.

Once you identify your key motivators, use them to turn your attention toward being creative, to actively engage your photography practice. Use motivators to help you find energy when you feel uninspired or apathetic about making photos. Everybody needs a nudge sometimes, and it's better not to have to rely on others to give you that nudge (like your instructors). When you are self-motivated, you know what to do to pick up your camera and become immersed in your meaningful work. Before you know it, you will be out there making more photos.

22

Time and Energy Management

Let's face it, you're busy. If you are taking a full load of classes, then you have to find ways to maximize your productivity within the constraints of your limited time and energy resources. You probably learned early on that to cope with the deluge of incoming assignments you need strategies to help you get those projects finished and presentation-ready, on time. One common strategy students tend to figure out is how to conserve time and energy by applying the *principle of least effort*: apply the least amount of effort needed to achieve the greatest results.

The principle of least effort applies to a lot of situations, especially if the assigned project isn't something that interests you. Things that fall to the bottom of the priority list usually get the least amount of attention. On the other hand, things that are at the top of the priority list, things that are important don't tend to fit within the theory of the economy of work. Things you care about or enjoy can make you want to invest more time, to go above and beyond what's required, because they mean something to you. When you are passionate about something, it can motivate you to put in lots of time and effort, to produce something you are proud of, a product that exceeds expectations.

You may also be willing to work harder because people are depending on you or you have high expectations for the result of your work. For example, you might put in more time when it will get you the A you want on an assignment. This chapter can help by introducing some effective methods and strategies for managing your time and energy, so you can schedule time to work on what you want to work on. When you want to attain the highest level of photographic achievement in your courses, begin with *time management*.

DOI: 10.4324/9781003106685-22

As a photo student, your life is full of demands on your time and attention. Your challenge is to figure out how to divide those 24 hours per day in a way that allows you to do everything that needs to get done. This is a difficult, yet attainable goal. Part of the challenge with your photography practice is that it can be time-consuming. For instance, think how long it will take to go from an idea to edited, finished images. How much time will you need to set aside per day (or per week) for your practice? And, how will you avoid all the fascinating distractions, random interruptions, and getting drawn into unexpected, time-draining situations?

One suggestion is to print out the file with seven schedule grids from the website www.photostudent.net > Resources tab. Each square in the grid represents one hour in a 24-hour day. The purpose of the schedule is to help you visualize the defined amount of time you have, so you can strategize how to best use those hours. This practice is beneficial, because it can help you see how the actions you take *now* will affect your *future* hours. The first step is to figure out how much time you need for your necessities per day.

Sleep	7–9 hours
Getting ready for your day	½ hour
Breakfast	½ hour
Lunch	3/4 hour
Dinner	3/4 hour
Classes	4 hours (est.)
Studying for other classes	4 hours (est.)
Photography	2 hours

This estimate totals at 20.5 hours, assuming that you get 8 hours of sleep per night. Seeing the math can be eye-opening. This total leaves 3.5 hours for other life-enriching activities, like sports, clubs, fraternities, sororities, texting, friends, Xbox, Netflix, and your other coursework. It's beneficial to take time to do those things, but set time limits for yourself so you stay on track. Luckily, there are days you don't have classes, so for those days you can block out some catch-up time.

Following a schedule takes the wonder of spontaneity out of the equation, but it is an effective strategy for getting control over your time so you can succeed in your classes. The reality of the situation is that, after you leave college, this will be your life. Your adult independence comes with a price. You need to get a job, which will consume at least 40 hours of prime time and life energy. You should also allot time to give attention to your family, friends, and social responsibilities. Figuring out how to manage your time *now* will pay off *later.* If you plan on continuing your photographic practice after college, you will have to include it in your list of priorities and set aside time in your schedule to sustain your creative growth.

In addition to the daily grids you could use an app, like Google Calendar, to keep track of your academic and life responsibilities. Having a master calendar is the *only way* to keep track of where you need to be and to keep an eye on all those assignment deadlines that are coming up way too fast. In each calendar box, make a daily schedule, or a *to-do* list and cross off items as you accomplish them. However, a calendar, a schedule, and other time management strategies can only be used effectively if you combine them with methods for managing your life-energy.

Your time is only beneficial when you have the energy to take advantage of it. This is why *energy management* is so important. Think of the source of your life-energy like the rechargeable battery in your camera. All the things you do in a day require energy from the battery. When you eat nutritious food, drink plenty of water, exercise, meditate, and get enough sleep, your battery gets recharged.

Daily activities like studying, sports, and even creative practices require lots of energy. Your creative mind functions best when it has ample energy to generate ideas. When you start out learning photography, you allocate a lot of brain energy to figuring out how to operate the camera skillfully enough to get the photos you want. You have to focus on learning how to use editing software so you can refine your photos. In addition, you will study a lot about topics, like critiques, light, composition, and color. The beginner's learning curve is steep. You need ways to work smarter, not necessarily harder. Use these tips to figure out how to maximize your time and energy.

Let's look at your brain's energy needs again. To illustrate the idea, when your mind is working on your classes throughout the day, it burns about 350 calories of the 1,300 calories that your body burns while sitting.[101] That's over one quarter of your energy when you aren't moving! Use your attention to choose how you want to use that energy. It matters a lot how and on what you allocate that 27 percent. Since creativity requires a lot of energy, it's helpful to think about how you can manage this abundant mental resource.

At some stage, using your camera becomes second nature. If you are at that level, you can move your attention and energy toward other aspects of image-making. At a certain point you will be able to free up mental focus needed to develop your creativity. When you are a beginner you may be very conscious about finding a worthy photographic subject. You have to make sure your lighting, vantage point, composition, and sense of timing are good enough to make an interesting photo. Last, you know it's imperative your ISO, aperture, and shutter speed are working interdependently to achieve a good exposure.

If all those things are happening in your head, there probably isn't enough mental energy to consider much else. Imagine what you could do if all of those photographic considerations happened intuitively and all you had to think about is how to make the photo more interesting, more creative. This is the level your instructor is guiding you toward, a level of knowledge and experience where all your energy can go into your creative expression.

Your energy is used in several ways. There is the physical energy you need to move your body, mental energy you need to think, and there are lots of different kinds of emotional energies. Creativity is a type of emotional energy, but all of these energies can be used to support creativity. When you need energy for particular thought processes or physical actions, your brain will automatically allot energy to that need, sometimes taking it from other systems that aren't in use.

For example, if you are riding a bike across campus, some mental energy may be reassigned to your muscles to supplement the physical energy you need. On the other hand, when you are sitting in a room taking a quiz, your mind demands extra energy which may be diverted from other physical or mental sources. Your brain is amazing at figuring out where energy should go based on need.

When you want energy for creative ideas, or to go out on a photo excursion, it's helpful to plan ahead by considering where all that energy is going to come from. Prepare yourself so your creativity superpower will be able to work at full capacity. Eat a nutritional meal and get enough sleep the night before. You could also free up some mental energy that's being used to maintain a level of anxiety about all the things you have to get done that day. Because anxiety is a major consumer of energy, you can address it by writing a comprehensive list of everything you need to work on that day. That way, your mind no longer has to be anxious and fretful about forgetting what you have to do. You can let go of that anxious energy and send it over to the creativity power line. If you are hungry, eat a snack. Thirst? Reallocate that nagging energy of thirst by getting a drink. Free up whatever emotional energy is at the forefront of your mind, so your creative focus can benefit.

Successful artists learn to tap into chaotic forms of emotional energy and convert it to creative energy. Whatever good or bad emotional reactions you have, it's all energy that can be channeled to your creative impulse. Feel that energy of being sad, happy, disappointed, or hopeful, and use it to go out and make photos. Translate those emotions into visual images. What does frustration look like in a photo? How would you make a photo of joy? Let the emotional energy influence how you approach your subject matter. Use your DSLR or your phone camera, just get out there, and engage your practice. The photos you make are, literally, products of your precious life-energy.

If you are feeling a sense of panic right now because you feel overcommitted, like you've lost control over your time and energy and your commitments are getting away from you, call on your campus resources for help! Talk with your advisor or someone at Student Services to get back on track. They can offer additional strategies to manage your time and energy. Everyone needs help sometimes.

23

Make a Standout Portfolio

What photographers want most of all is for their photos to be memorable. They want their work to be considered relevant as part of the larger historical conversation about photography. If you are like other photographers, it isn't enough for people to look at your portfolio. You hope they will take time to look closely, understand the importance of the collection of images, and feel moved in a way that they will not be able to forget what they see! When they open your portfolio, you want them to be impressed, to have an experience like they just opened a treasure chest! To achieve this goal, design your portfolio for maximum visual impact, so it captivates while also giving information about your interests and what you are capable of doing with your photographic skills, knowledge, and abilities.

Part of the goal is to design your portfolio in such a way that it communicates aspects of your *brand identity.* Using your photos, layout, and presentation of your portfolio, you can influence the viewer's visual and emotional responses to what they see and understand. It's also much more than that. It is the impression they get from the sum total of your photographs, resume, artist statement, and all the creative pieces that serve as part of your portfolio.

Jordan Harbinger said that

> You have a personal brand, whether you are aware of it or not. It's the collection of what people know, think, and feel about you, and that collection

DOI: 10.4324/9781003106685-23

> is a result of your own thoughts, words, and actions. What we want to talk about today is being deliberate and intentional in that personal branding while remaining genuine and authentic.[102]

People around you know your brand. The question is, is that the brand you want to promote? People like Harbinger believe it's more beneficial to think about what you want your brand to be and then figure out what you need to do to market it and promote it.

By designing a brand around your strengths, you can build an identity that is marketable. When you have a clear idea about what your identity will be, intentionally design the marketing components that align with the qualities of the brand you want. Your goal is to control your personal branding by carefully choosing how you want viewers to perceive you, particularly in regard to the quality of your career portfolio.

The visual, conceptual, and technical quality of your portfolio elements will definitely leave an impression on a viewer. Viewers will quickly form an opinion about you and how you personally embody the attributes expressed in photos and marketing materials. For instance, your audience will quickly assign positive or negative labels for your choice of subject matter and your perceived level of creative and technical expertise. It's only natural that they will associate their conclusions with who you are. Photographers strive to communicate positive attributes, but you may also want your brand to convince others that you are capable, articulate, talented, highly skilled, dependable, etc.

The way you design your portfolio is an opportunity to produce a marketing package that establishes connections between the visual characteristics of what you produce and your favorable qualities as a photographer. In doing so, an effective portfolio will broadcast the kind of brand message about personal merits that future employers, business partners, and customers are looking for.

Help viewers understand your brand through the way they experience the level of quality in the work you include in two kinds of portfolios: a photography one and a career one. The way you choose to design your portfolios and the content you present will tell a story about your skills, abilities, future goals, your accomplishments, work ethic, and work philosophy. The purpose of these portfolios is to leave viewers feeling confident in your capacity to succeed. Your portfolio design should influence viewers in a way that makes them know you are the best person for the internship, job, partnership, assistantship, or graduate position.

The first kind of portfolio is the *photography portfolio*. This brings attention to your technical, creative, and aesthetic image-making abilities. The other, your *career portfolio*, serves to highlight more broadly your marketable skills and competencies. Your career portfolio gives a larger context for your photography practice. Together, your photography and career portfolios exemplify your highest educational achievements, along with your photographic and professional accomplishments.

Each portfolio should demonstrate the exceptional ways you are able to put your accumulated knowledge into practice. The portfolios, together, provide evidence of:

- your creative ability
- level of talent
- capacity for critical thinking
- technical competence
- writing proficiency
- quality of your work ethic
- problem-solving skills
- who you are as a person
- what you have learned
- ways you internalized your learning experiences
- results you achieved
- trajectory from where you began to where you are headed.

Your portfolios demonstrate the kind of sought-after proficiencies and competencies that the following 10 audiences want to see:[103]

1. Instructors, as part of course or program requirements.
2. Academic institutions (graduate programs).
3. Your general audience (followers).
4. Exhibition venues (galleries, museums, and online).
5. Curators, jurors, or gallerists (galleries, museums, and exhibition venues online).
6. Grant providers (committees, managers, officers, and agencies).
7. Nonprofit organizations (volunteer opportunities).
8. Clients (anyone who wants to purchase photos or hire you to make them).
9. Partners (business).
10. Potential employers (managers, business owners, committees, or human resource personnel in corporations, companies, small businesses, or academic institutions).

At the end of your college program, you may need to create several photography and/or career portfolios, each tailored to a specific purpose. Your photography portfolio can serve as a stand-alone marketing tool, especially where photography plays an important part in your career goals. A photo portfolio can function on its own, but it's usually included as a part of your more comprehensive career portfolio. Here are two lists of potential portfolio contents:

Photography Portfolio

- 10–20 of your most successful photos
- personal philosophy
- artist statement
- portfolio Information (includes numbers in order, titles, medium, exhibition size, and year created)
- artists of greatest influence (with links to their works)
- photography lineage (a family tree including you, your instructors, their instructors, etc.)

Career Portfolio

- photography portfolio
- resume or curriculum vitae
- exhibition list
- work philosophy
- a project you were part of: "a team or collaboration, that shows how you took a leadership role, and how the team worked together to solve a problem," suggests Rob Dickes (photo-educator, photographer, and the Chairperson for the Midwest Chapter of the Society for Photographic Education)
- diversity statement
- career goals
- skills and abilities (top five combined)
- references (three to five names, job titles, and email contacts).

If you are in an art program, you may choose to add an additional portfolio page to your online career portfolio that shows your best 10–20 pieces of additional creative media, like drawing, painting, graphic design, or ceramics. If you didn't make any portfolio-worthy pieces, then don't include the page. Never show below-par work.

Written documents in your career portfolio need to be organized, attractive in their design, easy to read, and grammatically perfect. Perfection is very important with written pieces, so seek out skilled proofreaders who will go over your materials. Contact your institution's Writing Center and ask for help. You may also have a Career Placement Office that houses resume and cover letter experts. Take advantage of your resources!

Each portfolio should be organized in a way that grabs the attention of the audience you want to reach. The portfolios should be clear in their purpose, so they can accomplish the goals you want to achieve. For instance, if you are pitching your portfolio to a gallery or museum curator, the photos you select will be very different from what you might show a potential wedding client.

The way you design and present your portfolios depends entirely on your purpose. "REMEMBER, PURPOSE EQUALS RELEVANCE AND IN TURN CREATES EFFECTIVENESS and the purpose for the portfolio dictates what goes into it and how you show it."[104]

Both kinds of portfolios can be presented in three ways: as a website, as physical artifacts, and as digital files. The method for how you present your portfolios is dictated by the requirements of the audience. Some job applications will ask for a link to a website, while face-to-face interviewers may request professional-quality photographic prints or a hard-cover portfolio book. They could also want high-quality printouts of documents like your artist statement and curriculum vitae. Be fully prepared for anything at an interview. For instance, bring a laptop in case they ask to see work not included in the hard copies they requested.

If you are asked to send photo portfolio files, find out about the pixel dimension and format requirements – for example, if they prefer pdf, png, or jpg files. Know exactly what your targeted audience needs from you. It's always best to have your career portfolio both posted on a website and as physical artifacts. Organize both versions in ways that are logical and easy to navigate. A well-organized, high-quality portfolio presentation communicates that you are professional, organized, and prepared.

Your photography portfolio should include 10–20 of your most successful images. Quality is far more important than quantity. If you only have 10 high-quality photos, only show those 10. Including over 20 artworks is not recommended. Again, the group of photos you pick needs to be purposefully focused on the desired end result. This is typical advice, but if you are submitting creative work for a job or as the final portfolio for a course, do some research to find out exactly how many images are needed.

Get clarification on the scope of the portfolio your audience wants. For example, interviewers for an internship may be looking for a variety of styles and subject matter, providing evidence of your versatility and wide range of photo skills. In contrast, graduate school admissions committees might be looking for examples of a consistent, unique style that explores a single concept or theme throughout all 20 pieces. Graduate schools may want to see evidence of your ability to delve thoughtfully, deeply, into a single concept or idea. In both cases, it is up to you whether you mix color and black and white, digital and historical process images.

Choosing which of your photos should go in the portfolio collection can be difficult. It's hard to know objectively which pieces are essential, that represent your best work, and which ones to exclude. You can't use grades as a criterion for your choices, because a grade may only represent your level of success for the required outcomes of an assignment and not the image's portfolio potential. For instance, you might receive a low grade on a photo made for a landscape project, but that same photo could perfectly represent your portfolio's common theme of abstraction.

If you don't feel confident in your ability to choose your best work, then get some help. Think of the portfolio-building process as a collaborative effort. Don't hesitate to ask for advice from instructors, other photo students, and even those in your extended networks. Get feedback from professionals at a portfolio review event, like SPE, Photolucida, Filter Photo Festival, FotoFest, PhotoNOLA, PDN, PhotoPlus Expo, or the Center review. You can find an extensive list of review events at http://lenscratch.com/resources/portfolio-reviews/

Tell reviewers about your purpose for the portfolio. Is it for a class, part of an application package for a job, or an application for graduate school? The more information you can give reviewers about your goals for the portfolio, the more targeted feedback they can provide. If you want to end up with a 20-image portfolio, show your reviewers 25–30 of your top picks so they can recommend which 20 to show.

When deciding on portfolio photos, make an informed choice, which means taking an account of the following:

1. Responding with your gut, pick your top 20 photographs.
2. Gather a jury of five trusted art/photo students and ask each one to pick their top 20.
3. Consider which photos got the best response in critique. And, out of those, consider suggestions that might improve any of the images.
4. Ask a few people in your CSN and/or PLN. It's not advised that you ask for the opinions of your best friends, romantic partner, or parents (unless any of them are master photographers!).

Once you gather all the suggestions, you will be in a good position to make an informed choice for your 20 photos. In addition to what you learn in this process, here are some points to consider:

1. *Content*. The content of the photography portfolio has largely to do with the themes and subject matter in your work. There are two possibilities for content. The first, mentioned above, is that your content is unified around a single theme, idea or genre, like people, landscapes, social justice, gender issues. The other approach to content includes a wide variety of themes. For example, some photographers may build portfolios that present a wide variety of subject matter like travel photos, commercial portraits, and landscapes.
2. *Depth of field and visual clarity*. Your photos should be in focus. The point of critical focus is where you intended it to be in the photos. If it isn't where a viewer would expect, or the images are blurry, then there should be a reason why. A photo that is intended to contain an area of sharpness and doesn't should not be included.

3. *Light and shadow.* The light portrayed in your images should support the concept and subject matter in the photos. Use your portfolios to exhibit your skillful use and understanding of light.
4. *Black and white vs. color.* Your preference of color treatment should support the composition, lighting, and subject matter. The approach you use is clearly the right choice for each photograph.
5. *Timing.* You captured the subject at the moment when it best expressed the story you are telling, or when it perfectly described the scene.
6. *Composition.* The way you arrange the visual elements in elements in the photos serves to invite the viewer into the frame, to entice them to explore, feel, and understand what they see. Composition is one of the most important ways to provide a memorable viewing experience.
7. *Concept or theme.* Can the viewer relate to or understand something about the photo, or does the photo leave the viewer confused? The viewer wants to have an engaging, unforgettable experience. Does the portfolio provide that experience?
8. *Visual interest.* A couple of design principles that come into play when considering the visual interest in the group of photos are unity and variety. These principles apply to a portfolio in the same way they function in individual photographic compositions. The expressions of unity and variety create visual interest. A viewer becomes more engaged when they notice the way elements (or individual photographs) relate to each other, yet differ in their own unique ways.

Unity is described as the visual and/or conceptual threads that run through your portfolio. It's the way everything is tied together. Your distinct style, concept, subject matter, or technical qualities are a few examples of approaches that can create a sense of unity in the portfolio. Variety is about how those elements in your photos are uniquely different. For example, a photo portfolio may be unified by a connecting theme, such as portraits. Or they could all use the same color format, like they are all either color or black and white. Yet there can still be variety in that the images represent a diversity of people, of assorted ages, backgrounds, and genders. The skillful use of these design principles serves to attract and hold the attention of a potential employer, curator, reviewer, graduate professor, and/or interviewer.

A few additional things to consider regarding your portfolios are the order in which you present your photographs, orientation, and the size of the artworks. The way you sequence the images in your portfolio has an impact on the viewing experience. An effective order takes the viewer through a story as seen through your eyes! A successful arrangement will hold your viewer's interest, while getting them excited to learn more about you and your photography. To design an effective sequence, begin by ranking your images in order of visual impact and importance.

Assuming you have a 20-photo portfolio, the number 1 choice would be the image you would want to represent your work if you could only show one photo. Number 20 is the image that you would take out if you could only show 19. When you finish rating from 1 to 20, take your second favorite photo and use it as the last image in your sequence. The idea is that, if you begin and end your portfolio with your best photos, the viewer will begin and leave with a good impression. Viewers will also be more likely to remember what they saw when the series ends on an image with impact.

Sequencing the remaining photos that go between the first and last position in the portfolio is also essential. To add variety, split up images that are very similar in composition, expression, or subject. If you have two similar photos – for instance, of the same subject – choose the best one and drop the other from the group. Bear in mind, even if your work concentrates on a single concept, you need visual variety. Photo website designer Alex Vita recommends that, "If you have other particularly strong images in your selection, spread them out evenly inside the portfolio/slideshow. They maintain the structure of the entire content, carrying the 'weight' of the other not-as-good images."[105]

Another reason why you rate your photos is because, when you create new photos that are worthy of going into the portfolio, you will remove the weakest images from the bottom of the group. Your portfolios are living documents. In other words, you are constantly updating, revising, and improving the content based on your level of creative and technical growth. As your skills, abilities, and awareness grow, so too will your portfolio.

When you decide on a sequence on your website, you don't have to worry about alternating portrait and landscape orientations. For a print portfolio, alternating orientations is not recommended – otherwise, the viewer has to periodically rotate the set of images to see the correct orientation. Try to group landscape orientation in one part of the portfolio and portrait orientation in the other. This helps provide a comfortable viewing experience.

Consider the size of your images, with both physical prints and a portfolio book. Large exhibition prints aren't appropriate for a face-to-face interview. Interview prints should range from 8 × 10 inches (20 × 25 cm) to 16 × 20 inches (40 × 50 cm), depending on your ability to transport a portfolio binder or a portfolio box. For instance, if you are flying to a meeting, then it's more convenient to bring a binder with 8 × 10 inch (20 × 25 cm) prints. If you are driving, taking an Uber, or riding a subway to an interview, and you feel you can manage a box with 16 × 20 inch (40 × 50 cm) prints, then go ahead.

The next consideration is to design and produce a hard-cover portfolio book. Think of your portfolio book as a bound set of your best images. Since your book is the ambassador of your portfolio, the quality of the book is important. When you choose a book producer, check customer comments for information on accurate color rendition, quality of the binding construction, and the weight and appearance of the pages and cover. A high-quality book should accurately represent your images, look attractive, and feel really good in your hands. A high-quality book is impressive as a professional presentation tool, especially during interviews.

The size and format of your book is your choice. Again, think about the page order you prefer to best showcase your artworks. Also create a mock layout so you'll know how many pages you need if you only place one photo on the right-facing side per page spread. Include an additional page, on which you should put your artist statement. Keep the amount of text in the book to a minimum, but do provide titles for your photos. You want your audience to spend time looking at the images, not pausing to read lots of text.

To create the book, you can use one of the many online, on-demand, custom book printing services, like Blurb, Shutterfly, Printique, or Mixbook. With book producers, there is a direct relationship between quality and cost, so try to get the highest quality available for the price you can afford. With some research you'll find a service with an acceptable balance between quality and price.

In addition, you could put together a leave-behind marketing piece that features a selection of portfolio images, composed to fit on one side of a 5.5 × 8.5 inch (14 × 21.6 cm) card or an 8.5 × 11 (21.6 × 28 cm) page. On the reverse side you can display your name, web address, and contact information. Make several of these pieces to give interviewers and to promote your work at conferences or job fairs.

Finally, you should be prepared to talk about your work, based on the information that's in your artist statement. You should also be ready to discuss where you are going with your photo practice. For example, what do you think you will be doing with your photography in five or ten years? If you make it to the stage of a face-to-face interview, you will likely have a short amount of time to talk about your practice. Reserve some time to ask interviewers what they think about your images and, when they respond, write down what they say. Taking notes tells the interviewer that you value what they have to say and assures that you will remember their feedback. Plus, it will support the perception of your brand, leaving the interviewer with a good impression.

24

DYNAMIC Titles

Just because you are a creative person doesn't automatically mean you are good at coming up with imaginative titles for your work. Inventing titles is a unique, artful skill that's challenging for many image-makers. Yet, it feels very satisfying when you do think up a title that feels like a perfect match for a photo. Like anything else, it takes practice. The more you do it, the better you will get. After all the hard work planning, production, editing, and getting photos ready for presentation, assigning titles is the finishing touch. This chapter will provide methods for directing your creative impulse toward the words that can enhance the viewer's experience of your images. Titles can do this by offering your audience a deeper connection with your work.

Consider titling as a step in your overall production workflow, because it's an essential part of your creative process. There are no rules for when during the process you should add titles. For instance, some photographers think up titles very early in their workflow, even before pre-production. In such a case, titles can serve as inspiration for future photographs or even a project that contains an entire series of images. For example, Cindy Sherman made a series of almost a hundred self-portraits as part of her series titled "Untitled Film Stills." However, the most common practice for photographers is to attach names as the final jewel in the crown, after post-production.

Some photographers believe that an image isn't finished until it has a name. That doesn't mean that you need to title every photo you make! Generally, you only need names for the images in your portfolio, the ones you exhibit, or enter in juried exhibitions. On a practical level, titles help you identify, organize, and

10.4324/9781003106685-24

inventory your photos. Any time you want to promote your photos, enter juried shows, exhibit, apply to grad school, or try to get a grant, you are required to provide titles.

The main reason titles are so important is because they have the power to enhance the viewing experience. Your choice of a title establishes a meaningful relationship between the words and the image. The title should have an intimate relationship with its photo, and together the two communicate something more than the name or the image could say individually. It informs the viewer by providing information that supports, but does not define or describe, the photographer's visual story. An effective title starts a conversation. It begins a kind of poetic dialogue with its image.

You can inspire a viewer to think about the symbiotic relationship between the visual image and the associated text. In this way, the viewer is encouraged to participate more fully in the experience. Successful artworks and their associated titles invite viewers to connect and think about what they see, feel, and understand. When brainstorming ways to engage their audience, filmmakers Billy Wilder and Andrew Stanton once said, "Don't give them four, give them two plus two." In other words, use titles to provide an opportunity for viewers to join in your photographic conversation, instead of using the title to give them a punchline or tell them what it is they are looking at.

A title could be one word or an entire sentence. Some photographers, like John Paul Caponigro, prefer short, minimal titles. Others like them to be long and either descriptive or poetic. Caponigro advises that,

> rather than becoming a master of language, keep it simple. While there are notable examples where this maxim [less is more, more is less] has been defied with success –singer/songwriter Fiona Apple titled one of her albums with a complete poem containing over four hundred characters causing a buzz-worthy stir which reinforced her reputation for being both poetic and eccentric – at a minimum it takes a significant flair for style or even genius to pull a stunt like this off.[106]

With titles, the number of words you use isn't nearly as important as the specific words you choose. The English language consists of 171,476 words. You just have to find a few that express something unique and thoughtful to accompany your images. Titles should be at least as DYNAMIC as your photographs! Here are some DYNAMIC suggestions for your creative titling process:

- ***D**ivert your attention*. Do you remember the practice of seeing that was discussed in Chapter 10 – active seeing? In that practice you learned how to bring your attention and awareness to what you perceive with your eyes. You can use that same ability to identify and acquire titles as they spring up all around you in your daily life. If you can divert your attention from your eyes to what you hear in the world around you, then you might notice titles appearing all around you.

For example, listen to what people are saying in conversations, discussions on the radio, in videos, or television. Perfectly applicable words can come from anywhere, even in your classes. Listen to what students, staff, coaches, and your instructors are saying. If you hear something that resonates with you, take note. When words or a phrase pops out and grabs your attention, immediately write it down in your sketchbook, on a notepad, or use Notes on your phone (if you are in class maybe you should use a physical notebook).

- *You can't think of anything?* The most common method for generating titles is to look deeply into your photographs and see which words come to mind. They could spark an emotional response. Maybe the work will trigger memories. You might even experience smells or sounds associated with the photo. All of this information is material for a unique, personal, and pertinent title. Don't judge what comes to mind – write it all down, make an inventory, and allow space for ideas to happen. When you have some words as raw material, try putting them together and see what you can come up with. Use an online thesaurus to expand on words you have, and start playing with their arrangement. And, if you can't find words that work, don't be afraid to invent words! Photography duo Gilbert & George have some interesting titles for their work, including *Metalepsy*, *Beardwalk*, and *Frigidarium*.
- *Notice the thoughts in your head.* Sometimes titles will just come to you out of the blue. It might be your creative muse, whispering in your ear. Listen and be prepared, and write those words down in your notebook. Don't make the mistake of thinking you will remember the title later! Even if a title comes when you are falling asleep, put your sleep on pause and take the time to write it down. You will be glad you did.
- *Ask for help.* Ask your classmates for advice. Get them to respond to your photos by giving you a single descriptive word. Ask them to tell you about any emotions that come up when they see your photo. They may respond with a full-length title for your photo. This can be a great way to encourage someone to engage with your artwork and help you see something that has, until now, remained hidden to you. Write it all down and put words together. You can return the favor by swapping photos with a classmate and giving titles to each of their photos. Sometimes it's easier to think up titles for other's images than it is your own.
- *Make associations between things.* Look at the subject matter in your photo and start thinking of words that are associated with the elements of your composition. Consider names, action verbs, subjects, and adjectives. Write down as much as you can, then think about how pairs of words are associated. Feel free to make poetic, enigmatic, and mysterious titles!
- *Invite a stranger.* Don't hesitate to invite strangers to invent titles for your images. Post images online and ask for help. Lots of photographers do this on Instagram. Sure, you will get some really awful titles, but you might also get one good one, and that's all you need. Crowdsourcing is perfect for enlisting intuitive viewers to bring insights to your titling process!

- *Consider other sources of inspiration.* Lines or words from songs, poems, scripts, or stories are good sources for titles. Sometimes you will discover words that connect with your subject matter or visual approach. Other times, hearing those words can form mental associations that prompt you to think of new titles. These sources can also lead you to ideas for future photo projects.

As you go through the above methods, there are some pitfalls to stay away from when titling. For instance, avoid words that literally describe or interpret the image. An example of this would be, if you take a photo in which the main subject is a tree, stay away from the title "The Tree." Also, it's advised that you steer clear of the most overused, clichéd title of all – "Untitled." It's advisable to stay away from all cliché titles, actually, as they can degrade the viewing experience! These kinds of titles, like "Let There Be Light" or "It's Darkest Before the Dawn," are common and overused. They come with too much historical baggage in the form of clearly defined meanings. Clichéd titles push the viewer toward those commonly understood meanings, telling viewers exactly what they should think about the photo. If you want to check your title idea against a good list of clichés, here is the site to go to: http://suspense.net/whitefish/cliche.htm

Museums and galleries wouldn't like you to follow this advice, but you can reserve the right to change a title at any point, if you come up with something you like better. Lots of people change their own names, so why feel like you need to keep a photo title forever? Maybe you need to take time away from your work and get some emotional distance in order to identify a better title for an image. As long as you keep a record of past titles, you should be able to update and change the names for your work. You are the artist, the creator of your work. You have creative license to do whatever you want.

Part 6

Career

25

My Photography Speaks for Itself. Doesn't It?

One of the biggest myths among photo students is that you shouldn't have to write about your work because your photography speaks for itself. It makes sense. After all, isn't the point of being a visual artist to communicate visually? In his book, *Get to Know Your Narrative*, author B. J. Cary emphasizes that it's common for artists to feel that "Art is typically made from intuition more than argument. Your heart guides your hands as your mind watches in silent wonder. So, what are you supposed to say about work that leaves you speechless?" Then, Cary points out that this way of thinking about your photography is nothing more than an "effective" lie. It is effective because it can sound like a good argument in your head, stopping you from investigating an unexplored, deeply rewarding verbal aspect of your creativity.[107]

Photographs communicate mostly about the story in the composition. That meaningful interaction takes place with a visual language that can only tell part of your story. Artist promoter Jacqueline Lara reminds us that viewers want to know more information than a photo can offer. For example, she says that "People care almost as deeply about how you create, as they do about the end product."[108]

It's important to make a connection with viewers by telling them about your inspiration, interests, and artistic choices. They want to know your story. Viewers want to connect with the person that makes the photographs they love. A statement is firsthand information that highlights the relationship shared between you, the work, and the viewer. Your words inform the viewing

DOI: 10.4324/9781003106685-25

experience in a way that can offer followers a deeper appreciation of both you and your artwork.

Remember the question I recommend students ask whenever they are expected to learn something? "Why should I care about this?" Alyson Stanfield, museum curator and educator says that "It's up to us to educate people about your art, and the role it can play in the lives of others."[109] As a creative image-maker you have the opportunity to speak to your viewers about what makes your photographs meaningful and to explain why they should care. A well-written statement helps set the stage for this realization, because it presents an authentic, convincing story about your inspirations and the creative vision that brought the photographs into being.

In order to understand some of the purposes for an artist statement, look at one of the most popular genres of streaming video entertainment – the cooking show. People are obsessed with cooking programs. Viewers fix their attention on chefs as they prepare ingenious delicacies. As they cook, they describe ingredients, recipes, cooking methods, and tips for serving an aesthetically pleasing plate. The conclusion of their story is the dish's final presentation and someone probably gets to taste it. People love them, even though most won't ever try to cook the recipes. Onlookers definitely won't get to smell the delicious aromas, or taste any of the food they see on the screen. It seems like watching this kind of process would ultimately end up being dissatisfying. Viewers get none of the benefits of the cooking process, so why are people so into it?

Cooking shows present us with drama, a compelling story that has a beginning, middle, and end. Viewers enjoy seeing the story unfold. Everybody gets hooked on vicariously experiencing how the chef transforms the ingredients through all the stages of preparation as a recipe evolves. They feel personally invested in how the final dish comes out and they are left emotionally connected to the chef and their creations. Because they have learned about the intimate and creative relationship chefs can have with the food that they make, viewers feel like privileged guests who have been invited to be part of a creative experience.

From the viewer's perspective, this is the same kind of connection they are seeking with you! It's through the artist statement that we are able to make that connection. The purpose of the statement is not to tell viewers how to feel or interpret your images, any more than the chef can tell someone what to experience when they taste the final dish. When the work is finished, it is up to the onlooker to experience the final product in their own, individual way. A statement helps teach viewers about your story, as told through your life and photography practice. At the same time, you invite them to gain a deeper understanding of your technological, material, creative, psychological, and emotional processes. This information will inform and deepen their experience.

A successful artist statement will facilitate a connection between interested viewers and the photographs, inspiring them to take the time to participate in a perceptual experience. If a viewer looks deeply enough into the photos, they will find meaning in what they see, feel emotionally connected, and personally invested. The artist statement offers an opportunity to grow that connection by inviting observers to be part of your inner circle.

Photographer B. J. Cary said,

> I truly believe that's why … the artist statement is such a valuable tool … because it takes the connection you have made with your art and it deepens it for the audience – it gives them that human element. A person made this art. What compelled them to make this art? What compels them to work as an artist? That's what people are looking for. I think on some level your audience wants to say, "Ah yes, me too!" Because they've already seen the work and said, "I love this." Now they are looking to go even deeper … You are suddenly more integrated into what they are creating and it becomes an internalized part of your identity. And it gets exciting … what they are making helps tell my story … an artist expresses part of the human experience that somebody else wasn't able to express. That artist statement is that bridge that helps them say, "Yah, me too!"[110]

What the artist statement should never do is abuse the relationship between the photographer and the viewer by providing instructions about what they should see, feel, or understand as part of their viewing experience. It's considered bad form to tell viewers what you intend for them to get out of your photos. If they feel like you have spelled it all out for them, they have no reason to engage with the work or imagine how it fits within their life experience. Instead, invite the viewer to decide how they would like to understand what they see and what it is about the composition they find meaningful. Allow them the freedom to react to and interpret your work as a natural response. As a result, viewers will feel more connected to you and further invested in your photography.

Another reason why writing an artist statement is so important is because it's part of your academic experience. While you are a student, you are expected to learn how to translate the visual language into a spoken and written language. Your instructors require you to think critically and analytically about your work. Writing an artist statement is part of that process.

There are also practical incentives for composing an artist statement. The next reason is that you will need a statement when you exhibit work, apply for grants or graduate school, and/or jobs in a creative field. Your statement is understood to be an example of your ability to be intelligent, thoughtful, and insightful. As such, it is a unique part of your marketing package that also serves as evidence of your writing ability. This is why it's important to produce a statement that is meaningful, readable, concise, and error-free.

The fourth reason why you need an artist statement is because your photography doesn't speak for itself, especially when it's speaking to you. As discussed in Chapter 12, your photography probably has much to teach you. The process of composing a statement helps you focus on exploring the depths of your purpose, your intentions, and what the work is saying to you.

The goal is to find visual clues that lead to hidden personal and artistic insights. Finding those insights is hard, because the mind puts up a lot of resistance when it comes to introspection. Yet, the effort will open up opportunities for you to learn about yourself. This knowledge will help you develop your projects at a higher psychological and emotional level. This kind of examination brings clarity about elements of your style, your thoughts, beliefs, and motivations for your photo practice. In short, writing an artist statement can point you toward a better understanding of yourself.

The fifth and last reason is that your statement prepares you to talk about your work. You can think of your statement as a condensed version of your artist's talk. At some point in your education, during a job interview, or while promoting your photography, you will have to give an artist talk. You may even decide to make a video of yourself giving a talk so you can post it on YouTube, Vimeo, and your portfolio website. Viewers enjoy seeing artist talks from the photographers whose work they are fond of. This is another opportunity to hook people and bring them into your circle of interested viewers: "Remember – your statement is about expanding your audience, about welcoming NEW people to your work, not keeping things static. You'll have plenty of time to give new fans and followers the grand tour – LATER, NOT NOW – you have to hook and convert them first."[111]

These five reasons for making your artist statement could also be seen as five benefits for making an artist statement. Start by collecting as much information as you can, focusing on what you want to accomplish with your photo practice and why. Here are some points to consider:

1. How did your photography begin (the serious photography, not when you started taking photos when you were aged 5), and how has your photo practice evolved? What were the obstacles or challenges you had to overcome?
2. Tell viewers about key aspects of your life story, especially events that served to inform your photography practice. Here are some topics, but be brief:
   - personal, family, or cultural experiences
   - popular culture
   - politics and social issues
   - psychology or sociology
   - literature and your reading
   - spirituality
   - other.

   Include information that is relevant as an introduction to the work (choice of media, processes, editing, presentation). Discuss what it is about the subject matter you choose that interests you.
3. Talk about what inspires you to maintain your photo practice (artists, artworks, genres of art, etc.).
4. If there are questions you are commonly asked about your art, consider answering them in your statement.

It's important to know what to say in your statement. It's also important to know what *not* to say. For a top 10 list of "What *not to say* in your artist statement," please look under the Resources > Artist Statement Tips on the website: www.photostudent.net.

Once you have some paragraphs of content you want to include, you are more than halfway to being finished. As you compose your statement, write in the first person and use language that's readable and simple. Stay away from overintellectualized grad school language (unless you are actually in grad school). Write like you are having a conversation with someone. Then, edit your statement down to one page or less.

If you are someone who has trouble writing, then turn to your PLN to help. Find out which parts of the statement they understand and what parts confuse them. You should also take advantage of your Writing Center and Career Center, because they both specialize in writing and can help. Ask your friends and instructors for feedback. You may have to go through several revisions to make it technically perfect, but that's OK. This is great practice for the many statements you will need to write over the next few years.

You will learn to increase the quality and depth of your statements over time. Your narrative will improve and become more compelling. Compose the last paragraph in your statement in a way that it will, as P. T. Barnum said, "Always leave them wanting more."

26

Advising for Success

If you want to be successful in your photo program and graduate on time, then you need a good academic advisor! You need someone to guide you through the fulfillment of your degree requirements, but you also may need a person who can offer advice from a professional perspective. It might help to talk to an advisor who can suggest courses that are not only crucial requirements for graduation, but those that can prepare you to achieve your career goals after college.

Talk with your academic advisor about your job target and get their advice for relevant courses, but also take a look at the suggestions in this chapter. Assuming that you would like photography to play some part in your professional life after college, these pages will help you navigate through the steps of collecting the knowledge, skills, and experience you need to launch your career path. That said, you should always follow the advice of your institution's academic advisor.

The goal is to design your college experience that prepares you for your future in a creative field, by acquiring the academic and on-the-job experiences that contribute to your becoming a desirable job candidate. One purpose for getting a formal education is that it can accelerate the maturation process as an image-maker and as a person. The experience also helps increase your base of knowledge in a variety of creative fields. In addition, you will gain a broader perspective about yourself and the world you live in. This intensive learning experience is the perfect chance for you to become exposed to a variety of interests, fields, and topics. If everything goes as planned, you will grow intellectually and creatively.

10.4324/9781003106685-26

To take full advantage of this opportunity, think about how the courses in your curriculum will support your photographic expertise while at the same time diversify your knowledge and skill base. In other words, photography may be the central focus of your studies, but think about how disciplines like English, creative writing, and literature could enhance your conceptual understanding and performance of photography. These supplementary courses use some of the same processes, practices, and language theories as photography. Photography and English even share scholarly fields in the study of critical theory, which includes semiology and hermeneutics. Whatever classes you take, think about how they can support your end goals.

Other kinds of courses directly reinforce and broaden the skills you use in your photography practice. Here are 10 suggested courses to enroll in during your undergraduate studies. Each has a brief explanation for why the course is recommended. Plus, there are two optional courses that can offer a subset of photographers important skills for their photo practice. Note that the courses are not listed in order of importance.

1. Video Production

Provides further study in visual language and storytelling through a time-based medium (with your DSLR and other cameras), creating story arcs, videography, video editing, the production process, audio, and screenwriting. You may also deepen your awareness and understanding of how to use light, especially with moving subjects.

2. Lighting

This course could be from either a photography or videography perspective. In both cases, learning about light is an essential, foundational topic for a photographer. Study the properties of light, the theory and techniques to purposefully communicate with your images. Most importantly, you will learn how to better use light while deepening your awareness of how light performs.

3. Adobe Photoshop™, Adobe Lightroom™, InDesign™, and Illustrator™

These applications are industry standards for creative fields. The more expertise you gain in these tools, the more marketable you will be.

4. Marketing

The basic reason for taking a marketing course is to learn how to market yourself, products, and a business, whether it's your own or someone else's. Learn how to use the principles, techniques, and concepts of marketing to effectively promote to others an idea, a product, or a brand. This field requires you to practice analytical and creative problem-solving by studying cases where companies succeeded and failed with their use of marketing.

5. Graphic Design

Pick up techniques for working with clients while applying the visual language of design. Strengthen your understanding of compositional methods that are used to communicate ideas through imagery, color, and text. Create your own brand and identity package, which includes all the marketing components like a logo, business card, letterhead, and packaging.

6. Website Design

Before you take this course, make sure it is focused on *making* websites as opposed to *coding*. Do some research on whether the course is code-based or application-based, like Adobe Dreamweaver. Visual artists tend to be more comfortable with applications like Dreamweaver, which is a design-based program that automatically generates the HTML code in the background. Website design is an important course, because every company needs people who have these skills.

7. Art History

Learn about where your work fits into the timeline of art history. Discover the artists who were the first to take approaches similar to yours, and others that took that approach and made it uniquely their own. Develop an understanding about how your work contributes to the ongoing conversation in art/photography while discovering artists that could inspire your practice.

8. Photo History

This subcategory of art history is more specific to your field. Learn who the influencers were/are in any given genre. Discover your lineage along the timeline of photographers whose work you find inspiring. In this course you are sure to find photographers whose work connects with your own.

9. Drawing

Drawing teaches you how to see with focus and clarity. Art professor Kit White says that "drawing transforms perception and thought into image and teaches us how to think with our eyes."[112] Some students are reluctant to take a drawing class because they feel they can't draw. But this is precisely why you take the class … to *learn* how to draw! Once you learn some techniques, you can apply those refined perceptual skills to your photo practice!

10. Social Media Marketing

The online career advice site The Balance Careers says that the most important, most sought-after skills employers are looking for are social media, computer (proficient with a wide variety of software applications), and problem solving.[224] Such skills are in high demand partly because everyone wants to increase their visibility online. To help you visualize what this means, think about the relationship between how many people will see your photographs in a gallery versus how many could see them online. Taking a course in social media marketing provides not only a highly marketable set of skills you can use to make money, but you can use those same skills to promote your own photography! If your institution doesn't offer this course, find one online.

11. Set Design (Optional)

If you are the kind of photographer who is interested in creating tableaus or building sets, then this course has what you need to enrich your photo practice. Learn how to use power tools for carpentry, and work with other materials to build the world you envision as a photograph. Photographer Jack Alexander says that

> There are a number of reasons I love implementing set design in my shoots. The first is the creativity. It's a really fun process to see something come to life, to have your vision advancing from just an idea in your head, to a moodboard, to assembling the materials and everything needed, constructing it, and seeing the finished product in a photo.[225]

12. Entrepreneurship (Optional)

If you want to start and grow your own business, then all the courses in this category are essential. You will learn to make a business plan, launch, and market a sole proprietorship. At the same time, you will find out how to find investors, hire employees, and how to succeed in a small business.

Some knowledge and experience you may not find in classes, so make a point to seek them out. For example, five skills you should learn before you graduate are to:

1. Build and maintain every aspect of your own website.
2. Photograph two-dimensional and three-dimensional artwork.
3. Mat and frame photographs.
4. Pack, ship, and unpack framed photos.
5. Install and deinstall an exhibition.

It doesn't matter which college or university you are enrolled in, or what your major is, your academic degree plan probably requires you to take lots of elective credits. This built-in, open requirement offers you the freedom to take classes *you* want to take. It's a perfect chance to find courses that support your career goals, even if they don't contribute to your declared major. If the above courses aren't part of your major or minor course requirements, seriously think about taking them as electives.

It's important for future employers to know which courses you took in college, but they are also very interested in what else you did as part of your college experience. It means a lot if you are productive during your summers. It's recommended that you take a class either onsite or online (check with your registrar to see if the credits will transfer). Or, take a photo workshop, photo assistantship, a part-time job at a camera store, or an internship for credit. In the end, these supplementary experiences add extra value to your degree.

Internships, paid or unpaid job experiences, offer many advantages to students. First, you get to explore a job you are curious about, to try it out to see if it's something you would like as a career. Second, you get on-the-job training that your academic program can't provide. Third, you may be able to make money doing something you enjoy. Fourth, you make valuable professional connections that can become part of your professional network. Fifth, you get a powerful professional experience line on your resume. Sixth, which is very important, is that if you excel at your internship you could get personal recommendations from established professionals who can vouch for your work ethic, skills, and talents. Recommendations are the currency of the job world and your internship is one place where you earn recommendations. Seventh, and most important, there is a possibility they will hire you. It's common for employers to offer interns jobs after they graduate.

The last piece of advice has less to do with your academic or professional life than with your personal development. It is to travel abroad. In his speech to incoming freshmen at Adrian College, President Jeffrey Docking said that traveling abroad is, "the single most important learning experience you can undertake in College."[226] It's true that there are few experiences available to you during your college years that can have more of an impact on your view of the world, personal development, and maturity than taking advantage of a semester-long study abroad experience. Even going on a shorter, two-week trip will have a long-lasting impact on your life.

According to researchers at the University of Michigan,

> the experience of another culture endows the traveler with a valuable open-mindedness, making it easier for him or her to realize that a single thing can have multiple meanings … seasoned travelers are alive to ambiguity, more willing to realize that there are different (and equally valid) ways of interpreting the world … this increase in creativity appears to be a side effect of experiencing difference: we need to change cultures to feel the disorienting diversity of human traditions.[227]

For a photographer, the opportunities afforded from a travel experience are countless. Even if you aren't interested in travel photography, this kind of trip makes available photographic prospects from which you can create a dedicated travel portfolio, which serves as evidence of your flexibility and your ability to adapt to any photographic situation. More importantly, a travel experience will accelerate your maturity process by teaching you about where you fit in the world. Ultimately this growth of perspective will bring new qualities to your photographic practice.

The purpose of advising is to design your educational plan by considering the end goal, which is to get a fulfilling job and to continue your photography practice. Whether you want to find employment or become an entrepreneur, you need to know what kind of skills, abilities, and experience will best set you up for success. Find out what employers are looking for so you can include those learning experiences in your college plan. Businesses want to see evidence that demonstrates the skills and abilities that will support their objectives. They want to be very sure that your skillset will be valuable to the company. If you want to start your own business, find out what courses will help you most. Whatever your end goal, discuss all of these suggestions with your academic advisor and see how this advice can be beneficial for your academic plan.

27

Become Highly Qualified

When you visualize yourself in the job you would most like to have after college, take into account how that career choice will make use of your strengths, life experiences, skills, talents, and the activities you would enjoy doing for 40 or more hours a week. Think about whether or not you prefer to work directly with people or if you would like to work alone. Talk with a career counselor and do some research to find out what kinds of positions currently exist in the job market. Pay particular attention to the skills, abilities, and qualities employers are looking for in a job candidate. For example, onetonline.org says that the thing top-quality employers are looking for in a photographer is *dependability*.[117]

In what way do you envision photography playing a part in your professional life after graduation? How do you imagine using your marketable skills to support you financially? Consider what you would enjoy doing, while at the same time know that a job isn't just getting to do what you want to do. Even if photography is the primary service you provide, most of the time you will be marketing, engaging social media, editing, and accounting. It takes a person that is self-motivated, persistent, patient, and driven to succeed. These behaviors could be described as core values. Whatever professional direction you decide to take, your choices will be influenced by your core values, or behaviors that are required to achieve what is most important for you in life. Here are a few deliverables you may want from a career. They are the need for:

10.4324/9781003106685-27

- financial security
- personal growth
- creative freedom
- autonomy
- job satisfaction
- relationships
- leadership/power
- adventure/travel
- job location
- recognition
- job stability
- expectations for a certain lifestyle.

If you learn about a career field you think is interesting, contact someone who works in that field and ask about what it's like. Find out how their job supports what they want most out of a career. Ask them what kind of background knowledge and experience are best for that job. Solicit their advice on how to become qualified. Ask questions that help you evaluate the position and try to get an idea if it could meet your needs and expectations.

To learn more, seriously consider job shadowing a person currently working in a position that interests you. Rob Dickes, Chairperson of the Midwest Society for Photographic Education, points out that

> Job shadowing is a great place to learn the real-world aspects of the job. For instance, you may learn that a freelance photographer may only be on a photo shoot 5–10 days per month, or that a large percentage of time and budget for a wedding photography is placed into finding more clients. Shadowing and internships are the best opportunities to learn the ins-and-outs of the job. Job shadowing should be more short term (2 days–2 weeks) while an internship is a longer placement (3 months–1 year). Shadowing typically will not pay anything while an internship may or may not pay. This often depends on if you are getting college credit for the internship or how prestigious the company is.[118]

You will find a comprehensive list of internship, job shadow, and career possibilities in Chapter 6.

Job shadowing could lead to a potential summer internship, apprenticeship, or a part-time job. It's also a perfect opportunity for networking, meeting people that can help further your career. Internships and part-time jobs in professions like matting and framing, camera stores, and other related fields are perfect opportunities to learn through on-the-job training. You get to experience a variety of aspects about the photography industry while refining your skills and abilities in real-world situations. Any professional knowledge gained will supplement your classroom/studio learning, and that enhances your formal educational experience. It also opens doors for networking opportunities and provides material for your resume.

Your academic studies offer the knowledge, experiences, and momentum needed to launch your career path. They provide opportunities to develop your abilities, to learn the tools most sought after by employers, and to acquire the connections you need to turn learning into earning. Over several years you should be able to gain the information you need to transition, step by step, into becoming a self-sustaining, independent learner who's qualified and prepared to succeed in a professional life after college.

To be fully prepared for success, you need to take into account your financial situation. For instance, the decisions you make about your life after college are influenced by whether or not you have student loan payments pending. If so, you may have to concentrate on the short-term goal of getting a job more than the long-term goal of finding a career. You might have to get a *stepping-stone* job so you can pay your bills. Then, from that job, you can apply to other, more desirable positions. For recent graduates, it's common to get jobs that are intended to be temporary. Those kinds of positions should be understood as the initial steps of a one-, five-, or 10-year plan to end up in a creative job that you want!

After all that advice on getting a job, you should also be aware that there are other possibilities for your after-college life. You have options! As part of your long-term plan, here are 12 possibilities for directions you can take after college:

1. Get a job.
2. Graduate study.
3. Fellowships, residencies, and scholarship opportunities.
4. Creative job market.
5. Broad job market.
6. Independent or short-term worker as part of the gig economy.
7. Self-employed entrepreneur.
8. Become a fine artist.
9. Work abroad.
10. Volunteer.
11. Take some time off to develop your portfolio.
12. Make a career in an unrelated, yet fulfilling field.

A fair number of photo students don't want to rely on photography as their primary source of income. For some, photography is a life-enriching activity that is reserved as a very personal, creative practice. Such a photographer looks for jobs that have nothing to do with image-making. They are photographers who produce photos solely because it offers a fulfilling, enjoyable experience. They make images because they have a deep-seated need to practice their creativity and don't want to confuse their personal work with a career. The rewards those photographers get have more to do with an intrinsic sense of purpose and gratification than the requirement to get paid for their photography skills. Those people generally choose to work in an unrelated field that can support their photography practice. For them the option of attending a graduate program may seem very appealing.

Once you earn your Bachelor of Arts (B.A.) or Bachelor of Fine Arts (B.F.A.) degree, you will be qualified to attend a graduate program. You may decide to continue your formal education by applying to a two-year Master of Arts (M.A.) or Master of Fine Arts (M.F.A.) program. Though the M.F.A is considered to be a terminal degree, you might want to continue beyond that program and apply to Doctorate, Ph.D. programs in art. If you would like a career teaching in higher education, or you'd like to take some time to focus on developing your photographic practice, you could consider graduate school. Completing an M.F.A. program gives you the credentials required to teach at a college or university program in the United States. Some other countries require applicants to have a Ph.D.

Graduate school can be an intense experience that exposes you to a wide range of ideas, perspectives, and people you wouldn't encounter if you were working on your own. Its academic and creative rigor is designed to help you develop the intellectual resources you may be looking for to further refine your personal photography practice. It should also be noted that many of these programs offer funded positions so candidates don't pay for tuition. In fact, students may also receive a monthly stipend. If you enquire about programs, ask about funding.

Fellowships, residencies, and scholarships are available to postgraduate students. Look online to find open calls for positions and apply in your senior year of undergrad. These opportunities could be for a summer or multiple years, and could be available anywhere in the world.

The wonderful thing about photography is that it can offer life-enriching experiences, while at the same time providing an income. Your knowledge of photography can even prepare you for other kinds of jobs. For example, the technical skills and creative problem-solving abilities you acquire in your photo program are directly transferable to many careers on the job market. If you are willing to use your marketable skills and abilities to serve the needs of your customers/clients, then you are already halfway to making your career happen.

If you want a job in a creative field, then know that the first thing an employer will want to see is the quality of your portfolio(s). Your portfolio is one of your most important tools for getting a job in a creative field. Your resume tells a potential employer what you *have done*, but your portfolio is evidence of what you *can do*. Your portfolio verifies that you are visually and technically competent. It is the showcase of your skills, abilities, learning focuses, and how you can apply hard-earned experience.

Employers are looking for highly qualified candidates who have an above average capacity for creative thinking, problem-solving, analytical thinking, and an artistic viewpoint. They also want people that are proficient with the Adobe Creative Suite and Microsoft products. Companies like to see graduates who are experienced with image processing, editing, file organization, digital output, and printing.

As mentioned in Chapter 26, you will become more marketable if you have a variety of skills. Walter Isaacson, Professor of History at Tulane University, said that

> I think in this day and age we've learned the value of combining many disciplines ... when you look at the technology revolution and the digital revolution you see people bringing together the arts and the sciences. There is music and math and that is exactly what Leonardo [Da Vinci] did.[119]

The 21st-century job market is looking for those who are able to offer a diversity of skills and talents.

A company is unlikely to hire you solely on your photo skills alone. But, if you are a photographer who's fluent with social media, can make a website, shoot and edit video, then your resume will rise much higher toward the top of the application stack. You become a more valuable candidate if you can deliver solutions to multiple company needs. For example, small companies typically look for people who can perform the duties of more than one job description. Become highly qualified by becoming proficient with a range of skills and it will eventually pay off. Remember: skills pay the bills.

28

Launch Your Career Path

A study carried out by the National Association of Colleges and Employers says that employers are looking for "career-ready" applicants who are highly competent in the following areas (ranked by number):

1. Professionalism/work ethic
2. Critical thinking/problem-solving
3. Oral/written communications
4. Teamwork/collaboration
5. Information technology application
6. Leadership
7. Career management.

Notice that two competencies tied for first place, professionalism and work ethic.[120] Academic programs present countless opportunities for you to develop a professional identity and a strong work ethic. These are two qualities you should try to develop during your formal education. Treat your instructors and peers with respect, actively learn how to work with others, complete your assignments on time, produce high-quality products, and go above and beyond expectations. These are all powerful habits that will make you a desirable candidate for your career path, no matter what job you choose.

Marshall Brown, a career coach from the College Art Association, says that you should develop a personal brand that communicates what you have to offer and what others (employers, clients, etc.) know you can offer.[121] These are the

10.4324/9781003106685-28

qualities that make you unique and make you stand apart from other photographers. Qualities that are important for a photographer's brand are:

1. Active listening
2. Communication skills
3. Service orientation
4. Social perceptiveness
5. Active learning
6. Originality
7. Influencing others
8. Establishing and maintaining interpersonal relationships.[122]

It's common for emerging photographers to get jobs in a wide range of professions while also maintaining a part-time, freelance business in the gig economy. For instance, you may work at a graphic design firm while also working with clients in your own weekend photo business. Or you may promote your own fine art photography by spending weekends marketing and securing solo exhibitions where you can sell work. Such an approach assures a regular paycheck while granting you the freedom to pursue your other professional/creative interests.

Rob Dickes suggests that if you need to get a job, consider getting a night job. That way your days will be open for freelance work and planning out all the details of your short-term and long-term career plans (mentioned above). It would also be prime time for applying for other jobs and going to interviews.

Working for yourself is another very real option for a career. In fact, "more than half of all professional photographers are self-employed."[123] If you have a strong work ethic, a vision for a business, and an indomitable entrepreneurial spirit, then you may be able to build a business from the ground up. Once you have an idea for what your business will offer, you can lay the groundwork by taking business/entrepreneurship courses that will provide the learning experiences you need to be an innovative, prosperous business leader. In these courses you will not only learn valuable instruction, but will receive practical experience and opportunities to make professional contacts, build relationships (networking), and bring business instructors into your personal learning network (PLN).

If you would like to take a path toward entrepreneurship but you feel like you are at a disadvantage because you don't have the money you need to buy professional equipment, just know that you may not need a large initial investment. Many professionals rent the equipment they need for each particular client's job. That way you can customize your equipment for each photo session, while keeping startup costs and overhead expenses low.

You may have your heart set on becoming a fine artist. Fine art is one of the careers least pursued by recent graduates. Fine art is a highly competitive field and this career choice requires an extraordinary amount of passion and determination. Being a fine artist falls within the category of entrepreneurship, but instead of selling customers a service you produce and sell your own products. Fine artists can promote and sell their work independently or through a partnership with a gallery.

It's tough, though certainly not impossible, to find gallery representation right out of college. Gallerists typically like to represent artists that come with a reputation and a high-potential clientele. An art gallery could consider recent graduates that have large numbers of active followers on social media and have a history of selling their work. If this is your desire, then do some research to find galleries where you think the aesthetic of your work fits with their collection of artists/artworks.

Set up some meetings to show your work at several galleries and ask questions such as how much commission they take (galleries usually take at least 50 percent of your asking price after a sale). If a gallery wants to represent you, then great. If a gallery declines to work with you, then that's also great. A negative response means your work isn't a fit for that gallery. Plus, the experience you gained in the process builds knowledge you can take to your next prospective gallery meeting.

Some students choose to work abroad for some time after college. The most common job position is teaching English in countries such as Japan. It's also possible to work as a photographer at a resort or aboard a cruise ship. You might be able to find a job assisting an overseas photographer or someone who takes people on photo tours around the world. These jobs are hard work, but full of photographic possibilities while traveling in other countries.

If you can afford to take some time off before jumping straight into a career, you could volunteer at a nonprofit arts organization, a photography organization, or an art museum. These are all prospects for on-the-job-training, growing your network, and learning in the field, all while staying connected to the photo/art world. Find like-minded people and organizations that can offer continuing professional development and valuable insights into new, unknown career opportunities.

Volunteering your time and resources is a good choice in some circumstances, but not in others. For instance, you may be asked by family and friends to voluntarily photograph everything from senior portraits to weddings. They assume that since you are a *student photographer*, you are willing to provide your time and talent at no cost. The assumption is that you work for images to put in your portfolio.

You might feel insecure about your ability to produce professional quality wedding photos or other kinds of products, but it's advisable *never* to do photographic work for free. Even a volunteer position at a museum is giving you something in return (as mentioned above). For family, friends, or other clients, always charge some amount, or trade services. Your skills, your education, and your experience have value. These are perfect situations to start practicing professionalism. If someone asks you to take photos or would like you to give them one of your images, say, "Yes, this will help me launch my career. Let's discuss compensation."

Rob Dickes underscores that:

> Working for free doesn't only get you a bad reputation as being free or cheap, but it also hurts the field of photography. As an example: it is very common for people to try and get the lowest possible price from a photographer because they have seen or heard of other photographers who charge almost nothing. As a talented creative, it is important that you (the photographer) educate the client about why you are charging the price you are charging. I explain that my costs are relative to my lighting, camera, other photo equipment, advertising, experience and value in the marketplace with other similar photographers.[124]

You should also consider the thousands of dollars that you invested for your formal photography education!

Photographer Thorsten von Overgaard also recommends that when you are asked to photograph for your free, or for your portfolio, decline the offer:

> Saying no will filter away the people who don't really believe in exchange, and you will eventually end up with 100% clients who pay for your work. And you know what? Paying clients are happier with what they bought than people who didn't pay for what they got for free.[125]

The next step is to produce promotional pieces to market what you have to offer to prospective clients or employers. Ask competent perfectionists to give feedback on your materials. Also ask for editing and proofreading. The first item on the promotional *needs* list is a business card. Presenting someone with a business card supports your professional image (your brand). It tells people who you are, how to contact you, and where they can find examples of your work on your website. Here is a list of other materials you will need:

- promo card takeaway (double-sided with your information, plus one or more of your photos)
- resume, or curriculum vitae (one page)
- cover letter (one page specific to target job application)
- exhibitions list (if you have exhibited)
- artist statement (one page)
- portfolio
- list of references (three to five names of people you asked to be references – include position titles and contact information).

Optional, but required in some situations, are:

- biography (of up to 250 words, written in the third person)
- personal philosophy (one page).

There are lots of resources online, books, and experts at your academic institution to help you prepare these materials before you graduate. As a student, you probably have access to counselors, advisors, and career coaches. Take advantage of these experts before you graduate so that your personal marketing tools are of professional quality. Also call on your institution's career services to learn professional etiquette, and practice mock interviews on the phone, with videoconferencing, and in person (one-on-one).

Once your materials are finished, put everything on your professional/personal marketing website. Do some research on other ways to increase your web presence and drive traffic to your main website. Building a significant web presence is a long-term project, but it is an important part of getting noticed. Be aware that when you apply for jobs employers will look at your website and social media accounts so they can learn more about you.

Your senior year is the time when you need to be proactive and take charge of launching your career path. Call upon your resources to help prepare the way for entering the professional world. Ask friends, family, classmates, professors, and others in your network to offer suggestions about who to contact and where to look for a job. Let everyone know you are available. Get your promo materials out there in the hands of people who can help you, especially employers. After you find some prospects and send them application materials, then always follow up with an email or phone call.

Get out there. Attend regional and national job fairs and don't give up hope. Finding a career can be a full-time job. Advisors at the Savannah College of Art and Design say that

> A job search can take a day, six months, a year or more depending primarily upon how hard you work at it. Other factors such as the state of the economy, the particular industry and/or company of interest and geographic preferences will affect your search, but you will be most effective if you start early and work thoroughly and consistently.[126]

It can also be a multi-year venture, so be patient and persistent. Someone out there is very excited about hiring you. You just have to find them!

Part 7
Advice

29

Guidance on Your Photography Practice, Assignments, and Critique

This chapter and the next provide a collection of quotes that embody essential advice from over 100 instructors, professionals, photo experts, and more. The knowledge herein comes from the experience of helping countless students discover their creative and intellectual potential. These contributors can empathize with your challenges and support your goals, because at some point in their past they were students at the exact same level where you are right now. As you read these words, consider yourself one of their students and bring them into your PLN. Allow their experience as teachers to advance your photography practice.

If you find a quote that you connect with, write it down and put it in your camera bag. Read it every time you reach for your camera. Use sticky notes to put quotes on your studio walls and on your refrigerator. Take photos of your favorite quotes with your phone so you can read them when you need inspiration. The more you read them, the more you will internalize their meaning. To get the most out of this advice, make reading these quotes a vital part of your photography practice!

For biographical statements of each person quoted, go to: www.photostudent.net > Resources > Bios.

10.4324/9781003106685-29

YOUR PHOTOGRAPHY PRACTICE

Roger Ballen

Making photographs is a constant uphill struggle. You are never fully satisfied with the images you make, so you have to keep making more. The more you make, the steeper the hill gets … Instead of documenting what you see, transform it with your photography. Find your purpose! Start with rabbits, old dogs … anything. But don't start with cats![127]

Bill Barrett

What do you care about? Make images that tell us something we don't know about you. And, you have to be in one of them.[128]

Scott Berkin

Storytelling is everything. If you realize this, a lot of things will become simpler.[129]

Michelle Bogre

- Be curious.
- Don't be dogmatic.
- Make images every day. Every single day.
- Check out and master every piece of equipment in your school's equipment cage.
- Become a digital ninja.
- Don't make excuses. Ever.
- Show up early to every shoot.
- Take risks.
- Learn about copyright.
- Take an economics class.
- Learn basic coding.
- Become a better writer.
- Read fiction.
- Watch movies.
- Look at art.
- See images on the wall, not just on the screen.
- Be open to criticism, but trust yourself.
- Have fun.[130]

Marion Brenner

You're not seeing form; you're seeing light. The forms are light and shadow.[131]

Frank Brown

Photograph people you are comfortable with. Don't be afraid to be that guy that carries a camera everywhere you go. And, if you don't have your camera, practice taking mental pictures. Play![132]

Noel Casaje

I think we can't expect our images to have an impact on others if they don't speak to us. The photos that we capture, they must impress us first. Composition and post-processing can be technical and complicated if you allow them to be … I use visual cues that evoke strong emotions and feelings within me. When the image speaks clearly to me and I can understand its story or message, then I know the creative process for it is finished.[133]

Kelli Connell

1. Make work that poses questions more than it gives answers.
2. Be in action! Artists can often talk themselves out of things, don't let thinking overpower your process. Get to work![134]

Gregory Crewdson

You have a story to tell and you are constantly working to reinvent it in new ways. The artist is doomed to repeat those stories over and over. It's a search to answer questions about that story.[135]

Jeff Curto

Know photography's history. Understanding your own work in our medium is related to your understanding of both how it fits into contemporary photographic practice and how it relates to photographers who have come before you. The photographic impulses of our predecessors could be a springboard for the decisions you make about your work.[136]

Sylvia de Swaan

Taking pictures is a kind of act of meditation where one needs to focus inwardly as well as outwardly. When I'm out on the streets of a foreign city, my camera hanging around my neck, I know that if I find that center within myself, I can make myself almost invisible, becoming at one with the scene that I'm trying to capture.[137]

Arthur Field

Photograph what you know, your life and your family. Tell me something about you. Photography should not be hard work. If it feels like a task, calm down and try to have some fun. Making photos should feel comfortable.[138]

Andrew Fingerman

Social media is a content-hungry beast. Use your photos to create an audience of highly engaged advocates.[139]

Joan Fontcuberta

Use photography to help negotiate your concept of reality.[140]

Ryan Gines

Study languages, ask questions, communicate, stay inquisitive, love yourself and one another.[141]

Nan Goldin

This is my reality. I've made a record of my life. Photography has really saved my soul … My advice to young artists is that they shouldn't do it if they don't absolutely have to. If you don't have to make art to stay alive, then do something else. It's art – it's not a job – it should be what you do to survive … Art must come from deep inside yourself, and how you look at the world around you.[142]

Nicole Gomric

Don't be afraid to show people who you are. Don't be afraid to be vulnerable.[143]

Susan Gonsalez-Smith

You are an artist. You have a voice. Do something with it![144]

Lyle Ashton Harris

Photography is better than sports because it has no rules.[145]

Robert Hirsch

Unexpected things happen … but such "fortuitous happenstance" can take you in a new potent direction … That's where the appeal lays. It really lets your imagination investigate things to the fullest, encouraging an ongoing exploration into the nature of picture-making. This forward motion of discovery is a good thing![146]

Lauren Kalman

You can't make art without awareness of the world you live in. Move out of your very narrow view and engage your community, be an empathetic global citizen.[147]

Kovi Konowiecki

It is important to remember that often the most beautiful and interesting subjects are those that are closest to you. I would encourage photographers to try to find beautiful and captivating moments in the mundane and everyday.[148]

Kerry Lee

Pursuing your passion for photography just might end up being the most exhilarating, frustrating, joy-filled, exhausting, communal, lonely, wholly satisfying goal you'll ever strive towards. Some days you'll literally burst with pride at what you've created, and some days you'll feel so heavy with self-doubt that you can't imagine picking up your camera ever again. Don't quit, this insanely wild ride is so thoroughly worth it.[149]

Joe McNally

While we're talking, about 10 million pictures are being shot, and most of them stink. In this visual glut, how do you make your pictures noticed? How do we get somebody who's visually jaded, which we all are, to pause for even a moment?[150]

Andy Mattern

I used to have a note on the wall by my desk that read, "Work begets work," as a reminder that even when you feel like you have no ideas, trying something is better than trying nothing. Where you end up is rarely where you thought you were going, and that is okay. After you have made something you want to share, prepare yourself for outside voices. Listen to challenging advice, and adapt, but do not be deterred. We have all heard this before, but it's worth repeating: expect a lot of rejection. Save those letters and make art out of them. One thing will lead to the next, and the next. Keep moving.[151]

Alyssa Maurer

Get really weird. You are in a safe space where you have professors and faculty who are there to support you. Fail a lot and learn about what it takes to be a better photographer. Don't do enough to get by – do what it takes to excel![152]

Arno Rafael Minkkinen

When you make great photos, bask in the glory of your accomplishment.[153]

Ana Mireles

Expanding your creativity can be done by changing a small thing from your photographic routine. Change the time of the day that you go out to shoot, go back to a place you visited in a different season, or walk the opposite way when you go out the door. New conditions or new places spark new ideas.[154]

Colleen Mullins

One of the best pieces of advice I ever received was from the wonderful sculptor, watercolorist, and whimsey-generator, Dolph Smith: "Work like your hair's on fire!"[155]

Mariah Postlewait

I would say that college students should consider doing a few things:

1. Look at and think about photography – of all kinds. Think about what it does and how it accomplishes it. How does context shape your perception? Take a look at ad campaigns and how they use images – what are they trying to convince you of? Are they successful?
2. Take a look at all the photos you've posted on Instagram and imagine you are a complete stranger looking at your profile for the first time. What do they have in common (colors, compositional elements, subjects, themes, lighting, location, etc.)? What do they say about you? Do your hashtags and captions support that message, augment it, or resist it?

3. Consider that subject matter and content are two different things. Come to terms with the fact that, regardless of your every best intention, you can never control the way in which viewers will interpret your images with any degree of certainty.
4. Images do things. So make your images with the knowledge that they will influence the world. Be careful, be critical, and familiarize yourself with the ways in which people have tried (or not) to change the world with their images. Understand the advantages and limitations of various approaches.
5. Issues of power are necessarily bound up in the production of any photography. Who is looking? Who is being looked at? Who is speaking? Who is being spoken for?
6. Write about your work. If that is challenging, try just doing 10-minute bursts of free-writing at a time. Keep a sketchbook and write down your thoughts and ideas and sketch out those that you can't put into words yet. Try looking at your own work from the perspective of another person and write about it again; then consider what's changed and what aspects of your work you give the most and the least attention. You'll be expected to talk and write about your work often for exhibitions and presentations in the future, so try to get the hang of expressing what it is you're trying to do.
7. Photographs always, constantly, and forever simultaneously say more than we want and also not quite nearly enough. As John Tagg writes in "Everything and Nothing: Meaning, Sense and Execution in the Photographic Archive" in *(Post)Fotografisches Archivieren: Wandel, Macht, Geschichte* (2016) that photography is, "at once, overprotective of meaning and – as nothing but a stain in the dirt – at the same time inadequate to deliver the desired message: always saying too much and too little, more than is wanted and less than is desired, effectively undoing the notion that meaning in the photograph ever arrives in all its fullness or can ever be exhaustively defined."
8. Be bold. Be brave. Be accountable for your mistakes and humbled by your accomplishments. Take pride in your craftsmanship. Be active in the photographic community. Challenge yourself and others through your work.[156]

Lorna Rockey

An old friend … once told me, "keep taking photos Lorna, even if you never see a dime for your art. What you do comes from your soul and moves people. A true artist keeps creating until the day they die – no matter what."[157]

Amanda Ruzicka

Being a confident photographer comes down to three things: education, practice, and experiences. The more you can get of each, the more confident you'll become.[158]

Emmet Sandberg

Trust the process. Embrace the chaos. Cultivate serendipity. Be open to the possibilities, so when something unexpected happens you can use it. Take risks and give up control.[159]

Leah Schretenthaler

Having writing as a studio practice is important. Creative writing can help a lot. Write in a journal. If you get stuck, write a new artist statement. Rewrite fairy tales, write a manifesto so you can learn how to describe things. When you write, remember that it's about simplicity. Try writing an artist statement and start X-ing out words until you get down to one word. Research that word. That word should describe your work. If it doesn't, take that word out of your statement.[160]

Brooke Shaden

To me, the solution to this problem is quite simple. If you never try, you never know. If you only imagine but never create, you have no chance of seeing what you are capable of. It is one thing to dream, and to dream big, but it is another thing entirely to make those dreams reality. If you keep all of that amazingness in your head, and it is your goal to make that a reality, then you are failing not only yourself but those around you. I believe that the only way to fail is to not try. If you try and do not succeed, that is not failure; that is progress.[161]

Cindy Sherman

- Try to forget everything you learned about making art.
- Find a group of like-minded artists or creative people to hang out with.
- Take chances with what you do, make things that no one but you will ever see, unless it turns out so good you want to share it.[162]

Zach Sutton

Be humble. You'll reach a point where you take a great photograph, and you'll think you've mastered the art. You haven't. Take advice from others and understand that you haven't taken your best photograph yet, and that you do not understand everything there is to know about photography.[163]

Richard Tuschman

Get enough sleep. Pay attention to what inspires you. Get into a routine of showing up in the studio and making images every day. Take time to reflect on and edit what you've made. Repeat. As for staying inspired, read some fiction! That really feeds my inner life.[164]

Jerry Uelsmann

Fantasy is always in a dialogue with reality. Photograph things for what they are and also for what else they are. Be open to an ongoing dialogue. You invent a reality but it is in dialogue with what you perceive. Your camera is a license to explore![165]

Jeff Wall

So the enjoyment that you have in art irradiates you in a way, gives you energy, stimulates you. When you then turn away from the picture, turn back to your everyday life, you take some of those feelings with you. What you do with those feelings – and any insight they lead to – is unpredictable. Some will become curious and want to know more about the art. Some will find that their curiosity is displaced from the art and goes into other domains and shows them that they can approach their everyday problems in more creative ways. I believe art does have a consciousness-raising quality, but it's not controlled. It's not determinate. Every person takes it in a different way. You never really know what an art experience that really moves you is going to do for you. It will emerge in unanticipated ways.[166]

Don Werthmann

It is OK to put a lot of time and effort into getting one final photo.[167]

Peter West Carey

While some photographers have commercial reasons for shooting what they do, and others have high aspirations while seeking critical acclaim, most of us are shooting because we love it. (Sometimes shooting is a mix of all three.) That is why I say shoot for yourself. Don't worry what "important" photographers, or anyone else, think of your photos if you truly enjoy both shooting and viewing your shots … you will get more enjoyment out of the art.[168]

ASSIGNMENTS

Claire Benson

Create the kinds of things that only you could possibly create. From your experience, your memories and dreams, your fears, fascinations, inner-conflicts, and curiosities; from all that you see with those beautiful eyes, build a world unlike any other.[169]

Ally Christmas

Always write down or sketch out an idea once you have it (on your phone, in a pocket-size notebook you keep with you, even on your hand!), because you may regret your forgetfulness later. Moreover, even if something has "been done before", that doesn't mean you can't bring a fresh perspective to it; paying attention to the smaller and more specific details around you can help establish a unique viewpoint through your image-making practice.[170]

Pat Ferrucci

That's how our brain works ... most things that happen in our brain happen in, like, milliseconds, right? We make these decisions. And that's because we're using cues to come up with what we think something is ... we're watching a movie, and there's some ominous music in the background. Immediately, we know something bad is going to happen, right? Those are the things that happen in our brain all the time. So the more we pay attention to everything and don't just let things go into the background ... the more knowledge we're going to gain. But the key, I think, is that change and betterment in these kinds of areas, it just doesn't happen ... It takes effort ... And unless there's that effort ... your brain's just going to make quick decisions based on what you already know. And you're not going to learn anything new.[171]

Linda Adele Goodine

If you could only make one last photograph, what would it look like? Go and make it![172]

Elizabeth (Liz) Graves

Understand your settings and learn to trust them. Make your edits in post, but if you can get close to perfect in the field it will make your life easier and make you a better photographer. That being said, follow what you love, and if you don't find your style right away don't get frustrated, because like anything it takes time and practice. Having a camera in your hand should always lead you to new discoveries and a way to see the world through others' eyes, while also opening yourself up to letting others see the world through your own eyes. Make each day with a camera an adventure and capture every memory you can.[173]

Cig Harvey

Cameras are just expensive pencils: What are you going to say? ... It could be about a life, it could be about things you don't understand, it could be a way to better understand the world.[174]

David Alan Harvey

All the work you put out in the world – on Instagram, in magazines, in competitions – needs to be good. Just make it good. It does you no good if you get your photo into The New York Times, but it's a bad photo and it has your name under it.[175]

Jon Horvath

If you have a relationship break-up or some other kind of big event in your life, use that as a starting point to take a few days and use that experience as fuel for your photography.[176]

Clara Lieu

See every assignment as an opportunity. If you treat your homework like homework, that's what it will be. If you treat your homework as a chance to push yourself, to create something new, ambitious, and distinctive, that's what it will be.[177]

Jason D. Little

Picking up your camera and taking random photos is fun, especially when one or more of those random photos end up being really good. But giving yourself a project to work on will help you define and refine your style and sharpen your eye. A project also gives you the chance to explore a particular theme in depth over an extended period of time, allowing you to create images that will be even more meaningful than the ones you create randomly.[178]

Jennifer McClure

We're all curious about something, and we all have passions and obsessions. Make a project about those. And be prepared to learn something, to find something new. I was a TA [teaching assistant] for Amy Arbus for a while, and she would tell her students that if the project turned out exactly the way they thought it would, then they had failed. Something unexpected has to happen. I wholeheartedly agree. It's so important to be open throughout the course of a project, to give up some control.[179]

Aly Nickerson

You will think perfection is the most important at first, but eventually you will realize the best photographers are the ones who break the rules confidently and bravely. Learn the rules so you can learn to break them.[180]

Heather Nowak

The process is just as important as the product. There is intrinsic value in every mistake, every missed shot, and every triumph over self-imposed limitations.[181]

Glenn Rand

When you get the photograph you thought you came for, it is time to start taking more photographs.[182]

Richard Renaldi

Projects create a frame around your concepts. [You] have to be open to let other voices contribute to an overall body of work. Your work can only be made stronger by helpful guidance and input.[183]

Barbara Jo Revelle

How do you figure out what you want to make work about as an artist, as a human being? What do you care about? Even in beginning photo class, students have to do these kinds of interventions, or disruptions, or performances as their first gesture. You're not supposed to get arrested but you're supposed to do something that makes you uncomfortable and make a little video about it. You can make it about anything. If you're a musician, you can do that. If you are concerned with your gender identity or who you are attracted to, you can make it about that. But it has to make you uncomfortable.[184]

Christopher Schneberger

The students who are going to succeed are the ones who come to expect more from themselves than their professors do. Find solutions rather than excuses. Instead of giving up when you run into an unexpected obstacle, learn to expect them and work on figuring out solutions to get past them or around them. Focus on how you can do something, rather than why you can't. When faced with what seems like an overwhelming task, it's easy to become paralyzed and procrastinate. Instead, break the task into smaller tasks that need to be accomplished. Now figure out the very first little step in the first task and just do that.[185]

Andru Stone

I stress the importance of research. I will research 100 hours before I start a project. Look at as much media as you can. Make photocopies of what you like, then tear them up and put them back together and look at your work in different ways. Become an outsider of your own work.[186]

Crystal Tursich

Create a network. Keep in touch with the people you trust, keep showing them your work, team up with them and propose something together, give them feedback, collaborate. You don't have to accept every opportunity that comes your way. Learn to say "No, thank you" when an opportunity doesn't feel right. You'll thank yourself later. Never give up. Even if someone you respect tears you down. Even if you didn't get the job or the show or the sale. Never give up. Of course, to contradict myself, explore all possible opportunities so you can learn more about yourself and your abilities. You'll find that you enjoy some things that you never thought you would and you'll grow in new ways. Last, a piece of advice from one of my mentors from grad school: exhaust every possibility in your work. Do not accept that the first idea or outcome is the best – use it as a jumping-off point for your work to continue to grow. Allow yourself to try the ideas you know will fail; this way you can clear them from your mind and make room for the new and better ideas.[187]

Rebecca Zeiss

Close your eyes and image your idea, see it with the third eye inside your head, spend a few minutes with it. Try to see if you can imagine it from multiple angles. (Then I have them draw thumbnails of what they saw … next step of exercise is Go Fish. Tell three people in the room your idea and have them draw what they imagine or they can describe it and you draw it).[188]

CRITIQUE

Frank Geiser

Find someone who gives a shit and will tell you what's going wrong with your photography. Photo is really broad so don't limit yourself to doing only one thing just because you think you have to.[189]

Norma Santaolaya

Produce a lot of work even if it's bad. Eventually good work will start coming through. Critique can seem scary but pay most attention to the things people say about what you need to do to improve rather than what they say they like.[190]

Heather Stratton

Don't keep your work precious to you. Share it with others to get feedback, and when something isn't working the way you want to communicate … learn to let it go. Letting go and starting over (or just never stopping in the first place!) is imperative to artistic success. I teach my beginning students to understand the difference between being attached to the thing they are photographing vs. the photograph itself. Sometimes we give too much emotional weight to a photo because of the subject or the idea behind it. Doing that can cause creative frustration if you don't keep shooting and growing your ideas. Allow your ideas to take side roads into new projects.

Nobody wishes they had less time to get something done; we all wish we had more time. That extra time can't be found at the end of your project/task, it can be found at the beginning.[191]

Vincent Versace

Don't worry about what others think of your work. Worry about what you think of your work.[192]

30

Essential Advice on Career, Tools, and Mentors

This last chapter of the book continues with essential advice on your career path, photography tools, and mentors/teachers. The advice below will help you think about and clarify your academic and career goals. The wisdom given here comes from real-world knowledge from experts in the business and education of photography. You will also find advice from renowned authors and accomplished students.

The purpose of these words is to direct, encourage, influence, and offer realizations that can only come from hard-earned experience. These quotes are intended to deliver critical information needed for success on your creative path. If you read advice that seems helpful, take a chance and try it out. It could be exactly the support you need as you navigate your way through the learning levels that lead toward mastery in your photography practice.

CAREER/BUSINESS

Walid Azami

The true art is not only the final photograph but the process that got you there and created the artist. The photographer you wish to become is a product of the road traveled and how you react to "setbacks." Art is in the process also, and I urge you to take it easy on yourself! Start that project, launch the website, refer to yourself as a professional photographer, ask for your rate, learn a new lighting setup, ask that model to shoot, etc. Just start.[193]

10.4324/9781003106685-30

Greg Banks

If you don't wake up every morning and get excited about making art, go get a degree in something else! The reward is not necessarily monetary, it is in the making. If you are struggling to make art while in school, what happens when no one is around pushing you? This is a hard life if you aren't committed, but a great one if you are.[194]

Miles Bergstrom

Collaborate, Collaborate, Collaborate. Surround yourself with other creative people. I know you have heard this a million times but it's essential to your sanity as a creative. These people don't have to be videographers or photographers; they can be artists, designers, architects, etc. etc. You get the picture. While you do want to utilize other creatives in your field, I found it good to go outside that bubble as well. The folks outside the bubble will give you honest feedback, they have no ties to the techniques used or the way you shot something. They are there to look at your work subjectively and give you good honest feedback. Again, those other friends you have in your field – utilize them for the technical aspects of feedback.[195]

Petra Collins

When you're young, you have to watch your back and make sure people take you seriously. Even now, as a professional photographer who's been shooting for almost 10 years, it's still hard to command respect because I'm young and a woman. You have to play up being a boss and being sure of yourself. I feel like one of the biggest "life hacks," honestly, is just to not quit. That's the difference between someone who's going to be successful and someone who isn't: patience.[196]

Patrick Cone

Having face-to-face conversations and building personal relationships shouldn't be underestimated ... Reputation is everything: it's crucial that other people have trusted the work that you do. Plus, having a positive attitude and energy is important, too.[197]

Catherine Edelman

I would say, being personable is half the battle. When I meet someone and enjoy having a conversation with them, that's when I'll take a moment to look up their work. Because for me, it all has to be there: you have to have a vision, the work has to be powerful, it has to have deep meaning, and I have to enjoy working with you. The people who are successful, they're the full package. So work on becoming the full package.[198]

Angela Faris Belt

I strongly advocate to image makers the necessity of incorporating interdisciplinary studies into your practice. I cannot emphasize enough the importance of carefully reading … any book relevant to your field of study and thoughtfully researching any work about subjects that ignite your passion. Be inquisitive; be willing to explore. Don't limit your research to direct information about your subject; look into how it influences or is influenced by broader cultural history, religion, philosophy, politics, science, social sciences, literature, photography, and other arts. Seek out information shared by others who are passionate about similar subjects to the point that they have researched and studied, written or made art about it. Using an interdisciplinary approach to understanding your subject is a photographer's best asset; it informs your work in ways that visual exploration alone cannot.[199]

BJ Cary

Learn at least SOME business marketing. A clear message about why you do what you do will go a long way, no matter what aspect of photography you focus on.[200]

Dana Fritz

Cultivate curiosity. Ask questions. Keep in mind that questions are often more useful and inspiring than answers. Surround yourself with people who will challenge and support you. Challenge and support the people in this network you have created. Learn to love learning because it doesn't end when you graduate. That's just the beginning.[201]

Larry Gawel

This all depends on where you want to be in ten years. Do you want to be making art? Then you should be worrying about concept and content. And you better be aware of who else is making what because there is a lot of competition. You should know everything that's out there. But, if you want to be a commercial photographer, it's lighting. Everyone has a good camera now but not many people are setting up lights and learning how to use them. Lighting is where it's at![202]

Chase Jarvis

Congrats! You did it – you're graduating! … Graduation is the first day of the rest of your life. Learning doesn't end when you're no longer in the classroom. This might be seen like an obvious thing, yet so many people leave school and forget that they need to be great at their skill and instead get consumed by the myriad of OTHER things surrounding a career, such as building a website, getting a job, or trying to schmooze potential clients/bosses/peers … If you're coming out of school, you've just scratched the surface of what your craft is. Keep track of how much time you're allocating to various activities and make sure there is always time carved out to keep learning, growing, and evolving your craft.[203]

Lance Keimig

Learn how to network – not how to schmooze, but how to genuinely connect and communicate with people. Collaborate ... Collaboration with [others] is so much more fun than competing against your peers.[204]

Debra Klomp Ching

Photographers need to ask themselves, objectively, if their work has a strong concept and aesthetic, excellent execution of craft and originality of vision. Are they committed to making new work? Are they ready and able to continue to invest in themselves and their work? Is making photographs their primary passion? Do they understand that making the work is only about 50% of the equation? The remaining 50% is about the business of the image: marketing, public relations, record-keeping, fulfilling print orders, etc.[205]

Margaret LeJeune

Don't be shy about taking a chance. Make a call, send an email and collaborate with people in other fields. I connected with an African painter to make videos. This has changed the direction of my work. Follow what you are passionate about. Don't be intimidated because no matter what, you will learn. And that's exciting![206]

Glenna Jennings

Learn to balance the insights and experiences that come from both "The One" (you) and "The Many" (others). Nurture your own creative visions, but seek inspiration from a variety of sources. Learn how to create, implement and sustain personal projects, but consider the benefits of collaborative opportunities. Know what makes your vision unique by developing long-term, open-ended questions about your work and fearlessly following where this curiosity may lead. The camera is just a tool for navigating your world view and communicating your visual experiences of place and space, self and other. Our world of art and photography is small but powerful. Going it alone is challenging and, as the saying goes, "comparison is the thief of joy." Become an active member of your creative community so that you can learn to celebrate both your own successes and those of others.[207]

Dennis Keeley

It is an achievement to take your files all the way through to a print.[208]

Mark Klett

We need a sense of community now more than ever, so let's support each other. This isn't a sprint, it's a long-term gain. Whatever happens, keep making work.[209]

Honey Lazar

Don't be in a hurry. Respect the long game of photography remembering to build a network of support and guidance, because community is as important as photographing daily. Seize every opportunity to attend workshops and reviews for the exposure to learning and broadening your community. Expect rejection knowing its part of the process. Most of all, have fun.[210]

Ginger Livingston

Two things you should always do as a photographer: never undersell yourself and always find ways to give. You'll always get a good night's sleep this way.[211]

Steve McCurry

If you want to be a photographer, first leave home.[212]

Nate Mathews

Spend time looking at work you admire, which means you need to expose yourself to a variety of artists' works, and not just on the screen but look at photo books. I like to look at my favorite artists' work right before I head out the door to photograph. Also, turn off the distractions (TV, video games, social media) and turn on your passion for photography. If you can dedicate all your spare time to photography while you are in school, you might have the right career and a good chance of making it after you graduate.[213]

Madison Miller

Go out to observe and absorb as much as you can. Go to as many lectures as you can. Look at as much artwork as you can – all kinds of artwork. Get out there and socialize and make connections in and outside the classroom.[214]

David Ondrik

You get there by working, by failing, by listening, by trying again, by failing again, having some cupcakes (or bourbon) and assessing that failure again, by continuing to work.[215]

John Scott

Don't be afraid to ask if you can help work on a project for a new experience. And don't be afraid of knowing your value.[216]

Gerald Slota

The first rule of photography is, it's a small world so be nice to everyone. You never know where you will be or where your photography will take you or who will be in a position to help you along the way.[217]

Stan Strembicki

No one ever learned photography by sitting around drinking coffee, smoking cigs and bullshitting. You gotta get out there and push the button.[218]

Mary Virginia Swanson

Your website is nearly always the first point of contact with you and your work, and it must be perfect. Be smart about what message you are projecting on your website, and state it in the opening pages … Your attention to craft and presentation details will reflect the respect you have for your work and generate a stronger first impression.[219]

Aimee Tomasek

Interesting people make interesting photographs, that's why you have to take these General Education classes … become more interesting![220]

Dick and Barbara Waltenberry

Learn the photography business, not just how to take pictures. You need to understand file management, payroll, insurance, marketing, and accounting, even if you hire office help and an accountant. Communication with customers is critical. As you get started, listen to them to find out what they want. Your customers will tell you when they like and don't like if you ask them.[221]

William Wegman

Pay close attention to history and then forget about it. You have to have a background in where others have gone before … Then, at some point, you have to forget about it and follow your own muses and thoughts.[222]

Joel Whitaker

Advice for becoming a successful artist? My advice is to pursue that question for yourself. The process will take you to the answer, it will lead you to the answer for yourself.[223]

Lynn Whitney

The frame is a meaningful way to organize your thoughts and feelings of the world. And what you choose to include in it suggests something beyond the frame. In a "good" photograph, the world as it is, becomes tolerable, maybe even uplifting. Like the architecture of a church can be for some. Being a photographer and artist is an athletic endeavor. It takes practice and perseverance. Read fiction and poems and know who made this pursuit possible for you. Honor those voices as you continue to clarify your own. Remind yourself often that the roots of your interest in photography extend into those of the word: photography. From Greek roots, "Photo" which means light and "graph", which means to draw. When you make pictures, you are drawing with light. Finding success with photography is as elusive as the effort to fix light … which is why we probably are compelled to pursue it.[224]

PHOTOGRAPHY TOOLS

Megan Arndt

Know your equipment, backwards and forwards. Upgrading is always nice, but it's important to know how to use the most basic equipment first. Learn to study light, learn how to compose, and learn how to shoot well straight out of camera before falling down the rabbit hole of the latest and greatest equipment.[225]

David duChemin

Fall in love with the world, with her people, and the joy of travel. Learn to tell amazing stories and learn the technology behind sharing those stories. At the beginning I spent so much time and money on gear, and I'm not remotely your typical gear freak. Just get out there and make photographs. Your gear is probably good enough, spend the money on travel, not more gear.[226]

Angela Kelly

Fundamental to photographic seeing, making work with an understanding of how light itself transforms a subject, raises photography from the mundane to the visionary.[227]

Brian Matiash

Getting in the habit of always looking for a unique way to compose and present your photos is so critical. And my best advice to achieve this is to look differently … My point here is that looking at your scene needs to go beyond simply putting your face to your camera, angling it a bit, and pressing the shutter button. You need to take your time and think about the qualities of the scene in front of you. Ask yourself whether it'd be different if you walked a quarter mile away from where everyone else was standing … or if pairing an ultra-wide angle lens with an aggressive angle would yield a more interesting result.[228]

Jennifer Summer

You have to first know what you're trying to say with your photo. The camera can't read your mind. The camera will show you exactly what you show the world. That can be scary. We wear everything on our face. I started to think of my camera as another person with whom I was having a very intimate conversation. Sometimes, the camera is another me and I am "talking" to myself. Self-portraits have helped me express things I had been too afraid to acknowledge for years. There is so much relief in that. So much freedom.[229]

Peter Turnley

I've always thought that photography is not really about cameras, which are simply tools. Photography is about sharing – sharing our feelings, perceptions, observations about the world around us, with others and ourselves, for now and for all time. It is important to think about all that goes into making us the people that we are; what has influenced our vision, our passions, our loves, and dislikes – what drives our heart.[230]

MENTORS/TEACHERS

Steven Benson

A few thoughts shared with me over the years.

During a visit with Andre Kertesz I told him I was kicking myself about something I would have photographed but didn't have my camera. He just grinned and said, "Always remember – it is more important to 'see' something than to photograph it."

While picnicking with Jean Baudrillard in Arles (France) he said, "The photograph is not a document – it is a fiction." Arnold Newman once shared with me his now famous observation, "Photography is 10% inspiration and 90% rearranging the furniture."[231]

Simon Bond

Every field of photography will have its masters. In most cases, there will be more than one person you can approach as a mentor. Once you have decided on the genre of photography you wish to become good at, find someone who is already good at that, and approach them to be your mentor.[232]

Eli Campbell

What I like about SPE is seeing that teachers are also students.[233]

A. D. Coleman

Former students of the late Harry Callahan reported that, on the first day of the fall semester, Harry would take care of the usual housekeeping chores with his incoming Photo I students – roll call, lab rules, office hours, and such – before wandering around the front of the classroom making some terse introductory comments. Somewhere along the line he'd take a $100 bill out of his pocket, show it to them, and fold it into a paper airplane. Then he'd walk over to an open window and sail it out. "That's your first lesson in photography,' he'd tell them.[234]

LaToya Ruby Frazier

We make photos in the same way we live our lives and that should be in a state of curiosity. You should be accountable for the work you make. Mentors will come into your life and when they do, be receptive. When you are making work, you will hear their voices.[235]

Elizabeth Gilbert

Do you want to study under the great teachers? Is that it? Well, you can find them everywhere. They live on the shelves of your library; they live on the walls of museums; they live in recordings made decades ago. Your teachers don't even need to be alive to educate you masterfully … [but] there is this truth: No matter how great your teachers may be … eventually you will have to do the work by yourself … The sooner and more passionately you get married to this idea – that it is ultimately entirely up to you – the better off you'll be.[236]

Henry Horenstein

In photography, as in life, there are so many ways to look at things. Your teachers have their way, and that's what they'll be teaching you. But it's best not to get caught up in a single philosophy or solution, but to take a bit from each of your teachers (maybe even some teachers you aren't crazy about), mix them all up and find your own direction. Most teachers are smart and well-meant, but at the end of the day, it's your life, not theirs, that you'll be living.[237]

Mickey Strand

Being in the right place at the right time has put me in touch with lots of mentors and advisors. But you have to open yourself up to the comments and let your craft improve. At some point, you also need to take responsibility for your work and your growth.[238]

Notes

CHAPTER 1

1. www.cengage.com/discipline-college-success/csfi/, 12/21/20.
2. www.chsvt.org/wdp/Habits_of_Mind.pdf, 12/21/20.

CHAPTER 4

3. Grant, Adam. The Surprising Habits of Original Thinkers, TED2016. www.ted.com/talks/adam_grant_the_surprising_habits_of_original_thinkers?language=en, 12/21/20

CHAPTER 5

4. West Brett, Donna, and Lusty, Natalya. Introduction. In *Photography and Ontology: Unsettling Images*. New York City: Routledge, 2019, p. 1. www.academia.edu/37255219/Photography_and_Ontology_Unsettling_Images._Introduction,12/21/20.
5. Sontag, Susan. *On Photography*. New York: Farrar, Straus and Giroux, 1977, p. 92.
6. Modrak, Rebekah, with Anthes, Bill. *Reframing Photography: Theory and Practice*. London and New York: Routledge, 2011, p. xliii.
7. Heiferman, Marvin. *Photography Changes Everything*. New York: Aperture, 2012, p. 16.
8. NYIP Staff. Photographer's Spotlight: Philip-Lorca DiCorcia. New York Institute of Photography. www.nyip.edu/photo-articles/fun-stuff-for-photographers/photographers-spotlight-philip-lorca-dicorcia, 11/20/2008.
9. Quoted in Kevin Huver. Photography. 10 Quotes from Exceptional Photographers. www.kevinhuver.com/news/2019/8/19/10-quotes-from-exceptional-photographers, 12/21/20.
10. en.wikipedia.org/wiki/Philosophy, 12/21/20.

11. PDNedu 18(02), Emerald Expositions, New York City, Fall 2019, p. 36.

12. Fox Talbot, Henry. The Pencil of Nature. www.gutenberg.org/files/33447/33447-pdf, p. 40. 12/20/20.

13. Dilg, Brian. *30-Second Photography: The 50 Most Thought-Provoking Photographers, Styles & Techniques, Each Explained in Half a Minute*. Brighton, UK: Ivy Press, 2014.

14. Photopedagogy. Threshold Concept #8. www.photopedagogy.com/threshold-concept-8.html, 12/21/20.

15. Middlehurst, Steve. Context and Narrative, The Language of Photography, 7/4/2015. stevemiddlehurstcontextandnarrative.wordpress.com/2015/07/04/the-language-of-photography/, 12/21/20.

16. www.unm.edu/~jimstone/portfolio.htm, 12/21/20.

17. Archambault, Michael. PetaPixel, 20 Inspiring Quotes About What Photography Is, 6/19/15. https://petapixel.com/2015/06/19/20-inspiring-quotes-about-what-photography-is/, 12/21/20.

18. Hirshfield, Jane. *Ten Windows: How Great Poems Transform the World*. New York: Alfred A. Knopf, 2015, p. 3.

CHAPTER 6

19. Suler, John. John Suler's Photographic Psychology: Image and Psyche. Technical and Artistic Photographers. www.truecenterpublishing.com/photopsy/technical_artistic.htm, 12/21/20.

20. Sammon, Rick. www.ricksammon.com, 12/21/20.

CHAPTER 7

21. Wiener, Leni Levenson. We All Sew, What Is an Artist's Voice and How to Find It, 2015. www.weallsew.com/what-is-an-artists-voice-and-how-to-find-it/, 12/21/20.

22. Faris Belt, Angela. The Elements of Photography: Understanding and Creating Sophisticated Images, 2nd edition. New York: Routledge, 2011, p. 15.

23. www.wanderingaimfully.com/creative-voice/, 12/21/20.

24. Artnet. www.artnet.com/artists/joel-peter-witkin/, 12/21/20.

CHAPTER 8

25. https://en.wikipedia.org/wiki/Barbara_Kruger. 12/21/20.

26. Cronin, Matthew A., and Loewenstein, Jeffrey. *The Craft of Creativity*. Stanford, CA: Stanford Business Books, 2018, p. 31.

27. Cable, Jeff. Adrian College, Adrian, Michigan, Video Conference Presentation, 11/13/18.

28. The Abundant Artist, Why Connecting with Your Audience is an Important Part of Selling Your Art. www.theabundantartist.com/why-connecting-with-your-audience-is-an-important-part-of-selling-your-art/

29. www.adventuresportsnetwork.com/outdoor/vanlife/outdoor-photographer-travis-burke-is-giving-away-his-van-and-6000-of-gear/, 9/12/20.

30. Petrovski, Dzvonko. Lightstalking.com, 6/2/20. www.lightstalking.com/author/petrovskyz/, 11/10/20.

31. Reque-Dragicevic, Britta. Creative Inside Out, The Space Between Artist and Audience, 9/30/12. www.creativeinsideout.com/2012/09/30/the-space-between-artist-and-audience/, 12/21/20.

32. Email to the author, 12/3/20.

33. www.vivianmaier.com/about-vivian-maier/history/, 12/21/20.

CHAPTER 9

34. Elemental Life. 6 Reasons Why You Must Be Part of a Community. www.elementallife.com.au/blog/2016/05/19/6-reasons-why-you-must-be-part-of-a-community/, 9/8/20.

35. Senf, Rebecca. FotoFika Zoom meeting, 4/1/20.

36. Zamor, Riché C. What Is Community, and Why Is It Important? Ikeda Center for Peace, Learning, and Dialogue. www.ikedacenter.org/thinkers-themes/themes/community/what-is-community-responses, 12/21/20.

37. Kohr, Amanda. Wanderlust. How to Find Your Tribe. www.wanderlust.com/journal/how-to-find-your-tribe/, 12/21/20.

38. Hall, Karyn. Psychology Today, Create a Sense of Belonging, 3/24/14. www.psychologytoday.com/us/blog/pieces-mind/201403/create-sense-belonging, 12/21/20.

39. Horner, Garin. *The Photography Teacher's Handbook: Practical Methods for Engaging Students in the Flipped Classroom*. New York: Routledge, 2016, p. 60.

40. Email to the author, 7/16/19.

41. Florida National University. Why is Community Service Important? www.fnu.edu/community-service-important/, 12/21/20.

42. Our Community. www.unitedoutcomes.com/community, 12/21/20.

CHAPTER 10

43. Miller, Thomas H., and Brummitt, Wyatt. *This is Photography: Its Means and Ends*. Washington, D.C.: Garden City Publishing, 1945, p. 2.

44. Herman, Amy E. *Visual Intelligence: Sharpen Your Perception, Change Your Life*. New York: Houghton Mifflin Harcourt, 2016, pp. 11–12.

45. Conan Doyle, Arthur. *The Hounds of the Baskervilles*. Sweden: Wisehouse Classics, 2015.

46. Bell, Alexander Graham. www.quotefancy.com/quote/765396/Alexander-Graham-Bell-We-are-all-too-much-inclined-I-think-to-walk-through-life-with-our, 12/21/20.

47. Tharp, Twyla. *The Creative Habit: Learn it and Use it for Life*. New York: Simon & Schuster Paperbacks, 2003.

CHAPTER 11

48. www.chiotsrun.com/2010/03/21/quote-of-the-day-aaron-rose/, 12/21/20.

49. Hunter, Fil, Biver, Steven, and Fuqua, Paul. *Light Science & Magic: An Introduction to Photographic Lighting*, 4th edition. Waltham, MA: Focal Press, 2012, p. 4.

50. Lotto, Beau. *Deviate: The Science of Seeing Differently*. London: Weidenfeld & Nicolson, 2017, p. 58.

51. AnOther. Ten Weird and Wonderful Facts About Artist Caravaggio. www.anothermag.com/art-photography/9195/ten-weird-and-wonderful-facts-about-artist-caravaggio, 12/21/20.

52. www.upload.wikimedia.org/wikipedia/commons/4/4d/1602-3_Caravaggio%2CSupper_at_Emmaus_National_Gallery%2C_London.jpg, 12/21/20.

CHAPTER 12

53. Nemeth, Charlan J., Personnaz, Bernard, Personnaz, Marie, and Goncalo, Jack A. 2004. The Liberating Role of Conflict in Group Activity: A Study in Two Countries. *European Journal of Social Psychology*, 34, pp. 365–374. http://charlannemeth.com/wp-content/uploads/2017/03/NPPGBrainstormUSFR.pdf.

54. Coleman, A. D. *Depth of Field: Essays on Photography, Mass Media, and Lens Culture*. New Albuquerque: University of New Mexico Press, 1998, p. 10.

55. Lehrer, Jonah. *Imagine: How Creativity Works*. New York: Houghton Mifflin Harcourt, 2012, pp. 161–162.

CHAPTER 13

56. Sreechinth, C. Extracted Wisdom of Alan Watts, pub@ubtechglobal.com, 2017. P. 63.

57. Email to the author, 6/9/20.

58. West Brett, Donna, and Lusty, Natalya. Introduction. In *Photography and Ontology: Unsettling Images*. New York City: Routledge, 2019. www.academia.edu/37255219/Photography_and_Ontology_Unsettling_Images_Introduction, 12/21/20.

59. Burgin, Victor. *The End of Art Theory: Criticism*. London: Macmillan Education, 1986.

60. Paul, Richard, and Elder, Linda. *The Miniature Guide to Critical Thinking: Concepts & Tools*. Tomales, CA: Foundation for Critical Thinking, 2006. www.criticalthinking.org/files/Concepts_Tools.pdf

61. Conversation with the author at Adrian College, Adrian, Michigan, 8/30/19.

62. www.en.wikipedia.org/wiki/Pomodoro_Technique, 12/21/20.

63. Massey, Carissa. Notes from chapter review, 8/22/19.

CHAPTER 14

64. Sharot, Tali. The Optimism Bias. Time, 5/28/11. www.content.time.com/time/health/article/0,8599,2074067,00.html, 12/21/20.

CHAPTER 15

65. Austin, Eric K. Cinema and Public Administration Theory in the Classroom. 2012. *Administrative Theory & Praxis*, 34(1) pp. 114–119.

66. Finkelman, Joseph. How Many Bad Photos Does an Experienced Photographer Take in One Photographic Excursion?, 3/30/20. www.quora.com/How-many-bad-photos-does-an-experienced-photographer-take-in-one-photographic-excursion, 12/21/20.

67. Psychology Today. www.psychologytoday.com/us/basics/education, 12/21/20.

68. Psychology Today. www.psychologytoday.com/us/basics/creativity, 12/21/20.

69. www.susanmeiselas.com/latin-america/nicaragua/#id=somoza_regime, 12/21/20.

70. Dorn, Bruce. Be a Photo Mentor. Outdoor Photographer, 9/13/19. www.apple.news/Ai1GQkYpqRwGw3SOywSgoEg, 12/21/20.

CHAPTER 16

71. Angelou, Maya, quoted in: Ardito, Mary. 1982. Creativity: It's the Thought that Counts. *Bell Telephone Magazine*, 61(1) .

72. Ritter, S. M., et al. 2012. Diversifying Experiences Enhance Cognitive Flexibility. *Journal of Experimental Social Psychology*, 48(4), pp. 961–964.

73. Norgard, Brian. Thread Reader. Twitter, 10/21/18.

74. Cary, B. J. Get to Know Your Narrative. www.stitcher.com/show/know-your-narrative, 12/21/20.

75. Lehrer, Jonah. *Imagine: How Creativity Works*. New York: Houghton Mifflin Harcourt, 2012, pp. 6–7.

76. Wallas, Graham. *The Art of Thought*. Tunbridge Wells, UK: Solis Press, 2014.

77. Strathern, Paul. *Mendeleev's Dream: The Quest for the Elements*. New York: St. Martin's Press, 2000.

78. www/en.wikipedia.org/wiki/Oblique_Strategies, 12/21/20.

79. www.rtqe.net/ObliqueStrategies/OSintro.html, 12/21/20.

80. www.en.wikipedia.org/wiki/Lateral_thinking, 12/21/20.

CHAPTER 17

81. www.youtube.com/watch?time_continue=31&v=weIQIthC3Ks, 12/21/20.

82. www.truecenterpublishing.com/photopsy/decisive_moment.htm, 12/21/20.

83. Hirsch, Robert. Transformational Imagemaking: Handmade Photography Since 1960. New York and London: Focal Press, 2014.

CHAPTER 18

84. www.brainpickings.org/2011/06/20/everything-is-a-remix-3/, 12/21/20.

CHAPTER 19

85. www.apple.news/AhI1frz6STxqo4nBF0xkaAw, 12/21/20.

86. Fisher, Bill. 11 Tips for Location Scouting. Videomaker, 2018. www.videomaker.com/article/c18/8946-11-tips-for-location-scouting, 12/21/20.

87. Vila, Adrian. Taking the Shot is the Least Important Part of Photography. YouTube, 2019. www.youtube.com/watch?time_continue=40&v=Uduf0WkthGM, 12/21/20.

CHAPTER 20

88. Ansel Adams 1958 HD Documentary. www.youtube.com/watch?v=C1sNvguh3Y8. 1/1/21.

89. Kelby, Scott. Crush the Composition – Google+ Photographers. https://takhtesefid.org/watch?v=950789213887, 3/29/21.

90. Tharp, Twyla. *The Creative Habit: Learn it and Use it for Life*. New York: Simon & Schuster Paperbacks, 2003.

91. Gaiman, Neil. *The Graveyard Book*. New York: HarperCollins Publishers, 2008.

92. Sammon, Rick. Facebook Photo Therapy meeting, 6/5/20.

93. Babnik, Erin. Outside the Box: Advice for Making Risky Creative Decisions, Photo Cascadia, 2016. www.photocascadia.com/outside-the-box-advice-for-making-risky-creative-decisions/#.V9CgnGUSvoc, 12/21/20.

CHAPTER 21

94. Konnikova, Maria. *Mastermind: How to Think Like Sherlock Holmes*. Berkeley, CA: Viking Adult Publishing, 2013, pp. 22–23.

95. McLeod, Saul. Maslow's Hierarchy of Needs. Simply Psychology, 4/20/20. www.simplypsychology.org/maslow.html. 12/21/20.

96. Pink, Daniel. Drive: The Surprising Truth About What Motivates Us. New York: Riverhead Books, 2012.

97. Murphy, Mark. What Motivates You at Work? Forbes, 7/29/18. www.forbes.com/sites/markmurphy/2018/07/29/what-motivates-you-at-work/#3fff6a3d5c1f, 12/21/20.

98. Chodron, Pema. *When Things Fall Apart: Heart Advice for Difficult Times.* Boulder, CO: Shambala Publications, 2016.

99. www.hyperfitusa.com/hyperfit_usa/2010/12/commitment.html, 8/14/10.

100. Suler, John. The Psychology of the "Decisive Moment." Truecenterpublishing.com. www.truecenterpublishing.com/photopsy/decisive_moment.htm, 12/21/20.

CHAPTER 22

101. Inglis-Arkell, Esther. How Many Calories Does Thinking Burn? Gizmodo, 6/25/12. www.io9.gizmodo.com/how-many-calories-does-thinking-burn-5920970, 12/21/20.

CHAPTER 23

102. Harbinger, Jordan. Everyone Has A Personal Brand – Here's How You Should Refine Yours. Thought Catalog, 9/20/17. www.thoughtcatalog.com/jordan-harbinger/2017/09/everyone-has-a-personal-brand-heres-how-you-should-refine-yours/, 12/21/20.

103. University of Michigan, Stamps School of Art and Design. Portfolio Preparation. www.stamps.umich.edu/images/uploads/PORTFOLIO.pdf, 12/21/20.

104. University of Michigan, Stamps School of Art and Design. Portfolio Preparation. www.stamps.umich.edu/images/uploads/PORTFOLIO.pdf, 12/21/20.

105. www.foregroundweb.com/sequencing-portfolio-and-slideshow-images/, 2/20/20

CHAPTER 24

106. Caponigro, John Paul. How to Title Your Images. John Paul Caponigro: Illuminating Creativity, 7/6/12. www.johnpaulcaponigro.com/blog/8931/how-to-title-your-images/, 12/21/20.

CHAPTER 25

107. Cary, B. J. *Get to Know Your Narrative: Gain the Confidence to Write and Talk About Your Art with Honesty, Clarity, and Impact.* Papillon, NE: BJ Cary, 2019, p. 12.

108. Lara, Jacqueline. Why Every Artist Should be a Great Storyteller. 99u/Adobe, 6/13/16. www.99u.adobe.com/articles/54098/why-every-artist-should-be-a-great-storyteller, 12/21/20.
109. Stanfield, Alyson. Art Biz Success. www.artbizsuccess.com/, 12/21/20.
110. Cary, B. J. Know Your Own Narrative. Podcast episode 1. www.gettoknowyournarrative.com/2019/01/, 10/5/20.
111. Bamberger, Alan. Your Artist Statement: Explaining the Unexplainable. ArtBusiness.com. www.artbusiness.com/artstate.html, 12/21/20.

CHAPTER 26

112. White, Kit. *101 Things to Learn in Art School*. Cambridge, MA: MIT Press, 2011, p. 18.
113. Doyle, Alison. Top Skills and Attributes Employers Look For. The Balance Careers, 6/18/20. www.thebalancecareers.com/top-skills-employers-want-2062481, 12/21/20.
114. Alexander, Jack. How Set Design is Enhancing My Photography. Fstoppers, 1/31/19. www.fstoppers.com/bts/how-set-design-enhancing-my-photography-333932, 12/21/20.
115. Docking, Jeffrey. President's Address, Matriculation Ceremony, Adrian College, Adrian, Michigan, 8/18/19.
116. Lehrer, Jonah. *Imagine: How Creativity Works*. New York: Houghton Mifflin Harcourt, 2012, pp. 129–130.

CHAPTER 27

117. Summary Report for: 27-4021.00 – Photographers. O*NET OnLine. www.onetonline.org/link/summary/27-4021.00, 12/21/20.
118. Email to the author, 10/2/19.
119. Isaacson, Walter. The 1A/WAMU/National Public Radio. https://the1a.org/segments/2019-05-02-leonardo-da-vinci-500-years-later/, 5/2/19.

CHAPTER 28

120. Career Readiness Competencies: Employer Survey Results, 12/14. www.naceweb.org/career-readiness/competencies/career-readiness-competencies-employer-survey-results/, 12/21/20.
121. Brown, Marshall. Branding. Career Learning Center, College Art Association, 2017. careercenter.collegeart.org/jobseekers/resources/blueskyLMS/live.cfm?type=slide_video_presentations&course=146, 12/21/20.
122. Summary Report for: 27-4021.00 – Photographers. O*Net OnLine. www.onetonline.org/link/summary/27-4021.00, 12/21/20.

123. What Can I Do With This Major: Art. www.whatcanidowiththismajor.com/major/art/, 11/10/19.
124. Email to the author, 10/2/19.
125. Von Overgaard, Thorsten. *A Little Book on Photography*, 3rd edition, 5/18, p. 30. www.overgaard.dk/thorsten-overgaard-photography-lounge.html, 12/21/20.
126. Savannah College of Art and Design, University for Creative Careers. www.scad.edu/success/career-resources/resources/career-action-plan, 12/21/20.

CHAPTER 29

127. Keynote presentation, Medium, Midwest Society for Photographic Education, Lexington, Kentucky, November 1–4, 2018.
128. Conversation with the author, Medium, Midwest Society for Photographic Education, Lexington, Kentucky, November 1–4, 2018.
129. Conversation with the author, Constructed Realities, Annual Conference, Society for Photographic Education, Las Vegas, Nevada, March 10–13, 2016.
130. Email to the author, 7/14/19.
131. Green, Jared. Interview with Marion Brenner on Photographing Landscape Architecture. The Dirt, 12/10/18. www.dirt.asla.org/2018/12/10/interview-with-marion-brenner-the-art-of-landscape-architecture-photography/
132. Conversation with the author, Medium, Midwest Society for Photographic Education, Lexington, Kentucky, November 1–4, 2018.
133. Featured photographer, September 2018: Noel Casaje. Aperture Academy Photography Workshops. 2018. www.apertureacademy.com/guest-photographer-noel-casaje.php.
134. Email to the author, 6/17/19.
135. Keynote speaker, Constructed Realities, Society for Photographic Education, Annual Conference, Las Vegas, Nevada, March 10–13, 2016.
136. Conversation with the author, Medium, Midwest Society for Photographic Education, Lexington, Kentucky, November 1–4, 2018.
137. Email to the author, 6/16/19.
138. Conversation with the author, Medium, Midwest Society for Photographic Education, Lexington, Kentucky, November 1–4, 2018.
139. Conversation with the author, Atmospheres: Climate, Equity and Community in Photography, Society for Photographic Education, Annual Conference, New Orleans, Louisiana, March 12–15, 2015.
140. Keynote speaker, Constructed Realities, Society for Photographic Education, Annual Conference, Las Vegas, Nevada, March 10–13, 2016.
141. Conversation with the author, Conflict Resolution, Midwest Society for Photographic Education, Annual Conference, St. Louis Missouri, October 6–9, 2016.
142. Strant, Nina. Nan Goldin & JH Engström. Objektiv Press, 2/23/15. www.objektiv.no/realises/2015/2/23/photography-is-dead
143. Conversation with the author, Medium, Midwest Society for Photographic Education, Lexington, Kentucky, November 1–4, 2018.
144. Conversation with the author, Medium, Midwest Society for Photographic Education, Lexington, Kentucky, November 1–4, 2018.
145. Guest speaker, Constructed Realities, Annual Conference, Society for Photographic Education, Las Vegas, Nevada, March 10–13, 2016.
146. Editorial. Transformational Imagemaking: An Interview with Robert Hirsch, Inspirational Interviews Inspirations. Photo.net. www.photo.net/learn/transformational-imagemaking-an-interview-with-robert-hirsch, 7/18/19.

147. Conversation with the author, ThinkCatalyst Session, Integrative Teaching International, Kansas City, 4/5/17.

148. Roberts, Sarah. Portrait of Britain: Kovi Konowiecki on Photographing Liminal Spaces. 1854 Photography, 3/29/19. www.bjp-online.com/2019/03/portrait-of-britain-kovi-konowiecki-on-photographing-liminal-spaces/ 7/24/19.

149. Email to the author, from Courtney Larson, www.clickandcompany.com, 1/26/21

150. Harris, Mark Edward. Master Storyteller: Photographer Joe McNally, Digital PhotoPro, 5/4/19. https://www.digitalphotopro.com/profiles/master-storyteller-photographer-joe-mcnally/2/ 10/16/19.

151. Email to the author, 6/18/19.

152. Conversation with the author, Medium, Midwest Society for Photographic Education, Lexington, Kentucky, November 1–4, 2018.

153. Acceptance speech for Honored Educator, The Myths of Photography and the American Dream, Society for Photographic Education, Annual Conference, Cleveland, Ohio, March 7–10, 2019.

154. Mirales, Ana. 4 Tips to Get You Out of Your Comfort Zone for Photographic Inspiration. Digital Photography School. www.digital-photography-school.com/out-of-comfort-zone-photographic-inspiration/, 6/20/19.

155. Email to the author, 7/17/19.

156. Email to the author, 10/7/18.

157. McGraw, Michael. Local Artist Interviews: Creating Exposure for Minnesota Artists and Organizations Through Interviews and Networking, 4/15/11. www.local-artist-interviews.com/2011/04/lorna-rockey-photographer.htm, 12/5/20

158. Email to the author, from Courtney Larson, www.clickandcompany.com, 1/26/21.

159. Conversation with the author, FATE Biennial Conference, Beyond the Core, Kansas City, Missouri, April 6–8, 2017.

160. Conversation with the author, Medium, Midwest Society for Photographic Education, Lexington, Kentucky, November 1–4, 2018.

161. Squires, Megan. Photography Interview with Brooke Shaden. Clickin Moms Blog for Photographers. www.clickinmoms.com/blog/photography-interview-with-storyteller-photographer-brooke-shaden/

162. Bennett, Sophia, and Thapp, Manjit. Getting to Know Cindy Sherman. In *The Bigger Picture: Women Who Changed the Art World.* London: Tate Publishing, 2019.

163. Sutton, Zach. Fstoppers Answers – If There Was One Piece of Advice You Could Give a New Photographer, What Would It Be? Fstoppers, 10/2/13. www.fstoppers.com/originals/fstoppers-answers-if-there-was-one-piece-advice-you-could-give-new-photographer-what-would 9/14/19.

164. Gruenwedel, Stefan. Richard Tuschman's Tabletop Tableaux, Inspiration, Adobe Creative Cloud, 9/5/14. www.create.adobe.com/2014/9/5/richard_tuschman_tabletop_tableaux.html, 8/3/19.

165. Conversation with the author, Family Values, Society for Photographic Education, Annual Conference, Orlando, Florida, March 9–12, 2007.

166. Buium, Greg. An Interview with Jeff Wall. Believer Magazine, 2/1/18. www.believermag.com/an-interview-with-jeff-wall/, 12/5/20.

167. Presentation at Adrian College, Adrian, Michigan, 4/17/19.

168. Carey, Peter West. Photograph For Yourself Then Ask For Specific Advice, Digital Photography School. www.digital-photography-school.com/photograph-for-yourself-then-ask-for-specific-advice/, 8/1/19

169. Email to the author, 7/14/19.

170. Email to the author, 6/14/19.

171. Raz, Guy. Pat Ferrucci: How Does The Language Of Sports Journalism Reveal Racial Biases? TED Radio Hour, National Public Radio, 3/29/19. www.npr.org/templates/transcript/transcript.php?storyId=707192346, 3/30/19.

172. Artist presentation, Throwing Light and Catching Shadows, Midwest Society for Photographic Education, Chapter Conference, Louisville, Kentucky, October 1–4, 2015.

173. Email to the author, 2/26/19.

174. Walker, David. Quick Tip: Creativity Isn't Enough. What Are You Saying with Your Photos? PDN Pulse, Photo District News, 4/3/19. www.pdnpulse.pdnonline.com/2019/04/quick-tip-creativity-isnt-enough-what-are-you-saying-with-your-photos.html, 6/12/19.

175. Kraft, Coralie. Interview. "Life Looks Better Through a Viewfinder" – Mentoring and Wisdom from David Alan Harvey. Lensculture. www.lensculture.com/articles/david-alan-harvey-life-looks-better-through-a-viewfinder-mentoring-and-wisdom-from-david-alan-harvey, 4/12/19.

176. Conversation with the author, Developing Spaces/Places, Midwest Society for Photographic Education Conference, Peoria, Illinois, October 12–15, 2017.

177. Clara Lieu, Visual Artist and Adjunct Professor at Rhode Island School of Design (RISD). How to Be a Good Art Student, 12/20/12. www.claralieu.wordpress.com/2012/12/20/how-to-be-a-good-art-student/, 6/12/19.

178. Little, Jason D. 5 Pieces of Advice That Every New Photographer Should Know. Light Stalking, 3/4/19. www.lightstalking.com/advice-for-new-photographers, 6/20/19.

179. Kallianiotis, Niko J. Interview: Jennifer McClure, 3/23/16. www.nikokallianiotis.com/blog-1/2017/8/2/interview-with-jennifer-mcclure, 6/25/19.

180. Email to the author, 10/16/19.

181. Email to the author, from Courtney Larson, www.clickandcompany.com, 1/26/21.

182. Email to the author, 10/16/19.

183. Richard Renaldi: Building a Body of Work – At Aperture Gallery. Aperture Foundation, 3/31/19. www.aperture.org/workshops-classes/renaldi2019/, 10/10/19.

184. Conversation with the author, Medium, Midwest Society for Photographic Education, Lexington, Kentucky, November 14, 2018.

185. Conversation with the author, Medium, Midwest Society for Photographic Education, Lexington, Kentucky, November 1–4, 2018.

186. Email to the author, 6/15/19.

187. Email to the author, 6/24/19.

188. Conversation with the author, Medium, Midwest Society for Photographic Education, Lexington, Kentucky, November 1-4, 2018.

189. Conversation with the author, Medium, Midwest Society for Photographic Education, Lexington, Kentucky, November 1–4, 2018.

190. Conversation with the author, Medium, Midwest Society for Photographic Education, Lexington, Kentucky, November 1–4, 2018.

191. Email to the author, 6/25/19.

192. Kivowitz, Scott Wyden. A Photographers Interview with Vincent Versace. www.scottwyden.com/a-photographers-interview-with-vincent-versace/

CHAPTER 30

193. Azami, Walid. Advice for Every Photographer (As Far as Your Headlights Can See). Fstoppers, 2/18/18. www.fstoppers.com/originals/advice-every-photographer-far-your-headlights-can-see-219419, 11/16/19.

194. Email to the author, 6/18/19.

195. Bergstrom, Miles. Advice for Recent Undergraduates. Fstoppers, 6/16/15. www.fstoppers.com/originals/advice-recent-undergraduates-73354, 8/29/19.

196. Bauck, Whitney. How Petra Collins Went from Failing High School to Photographing for Gucci. Fashionista, 3/1/17. www.fashionista.com/2017/03/petra-collins-instagram-photography-interview, 10/11/19.

197. Behuniak, Tim. How One Photographer Reached the Top of His Field: An Interview with Patrick Cone. Fstoppers, 11/24/18. www.fstoppers.com/business/how-one-photographer-reached-top-his-field-interview-patrick-cone-310116, 7/18/19.

198. Kraft, Coralie. What Is Art Photography? Catherine Edelman Offers Her Opinion. Lensculture. www.lensculture.com/articles/catherine-edelman-what-is-art-photography-catherine-edelman-offers-her-opinion, 9/18/19.

199. Faris Belt, Angela, *The Elements of Photography*, 2nd edition. New York: Routledge, 2011, p. xvii.

200. Cary, B. J. Get to Know Your Narrative. www.stitcher.com/show/know-your-narrative. 10/1/19.

201. Email to the author, 6/18/19.

202. www.knowyournarrative.libsyn.com/011-interview-with-photographer-larry-gawel

203. Jarvis, Chase. Top 3 Things all Graduates Should Be Thinking About Right Now. www.chasejarvis.com/blog/top-3-things-all-graduates-should-be-thinking-about-right-now/. 8/25/19.

204. Crandell, Dana. An Interview with Night Photographer and Instructor Lance Keimig, 2017. www.blog.irixusa.com/an-interview-with-night-photographer-and-instructor-lance-keimig/

205. Lensculture. Insights from a New York City Gallery. Lensculture. www.lensculture.com/articles/klompching-gallery-insights-from-a-new-york-city-gallery

206. Conversation with the author, Medium, Midwest Society for Photographic Education, Lexington, Kentucky, November 1–4, 2018.

207. Email to the author, 7/1/19.

208. Conversation with the author, Medium, Midwest Society for Photographic Education, Lexington, Kentucky, November 1–4, 2018.

209. Conversation with the author, The Myths of Photography and the American Dream, Society for Photographic Education, Annual Conference, Cleveland, Ohio, March 7–10, 2019.

210. Conversation with the author, Family Values, Society for Photographic Education, Annual Conference, Orlando, Florida, March 9–12, 2017.

211. Email to the author, from Courtney Larson, www.clickandcompany.com, 1/26/21.

212. 121 Clicks. Steve McCurry – Inspiration from Masters of Photography. 121Clicks.com. www.121clicks.com/inspirations/steve-mccurry-inspiration-from-masters-of-photography, 10/4/19.

213. Conversation with the author, Medium, Midwest Society for Photographic Education, Lexington, Kentucky, November 1–4, 2018.

214. Conversation with the author, Medium, Midwest Society for Photographic Education, Lexington, Kentucky, November 1–4, 2018.

215. Conversation with the author, Medium, Midwest Society for Photographic Education, Lexington, Kentucky, November 1–4, 2018.

216. Conversation with the author, Medium, Midwest Society for Photographic Education, Lexington, Kentucky, November 1–4, 2018.

217. Conversation with the author, Medium, Midwest Society for Photographic Education, Lexington, Kentucky, November 1–4, 2018.

218. Conversation with author, Medium, Midwest Society for Photographic Education, Lexington, Kentucky, November 1-4, 2018.

219. www.mvswanson.com/wp-content/uploads/BJP_11-Tips-for-Building-Your-Brand.pdf. 10/30/19.
220. Email to the author, 6/13/19.
221. Stern, Katie. *Photo 1: An Introduction to the Art of Photography*, 1st edition. New York: Cengage Learning, 2012, p. 55.
222. Cloutier, Crista. The Working Artist Interviews: William Wegman Offers Advice for Artists, 3/17/14. www.youtube.com/watch?v=mVf5KsxNrsc, 8/17/19.
223. Conversation with the author, Medium, Midwest Society for Photographic Education, Lexington, Kentucky, November 1–4, 2018.
224. Email to the author, 7/12/19.
225. Email to the author, from Courtney Larson, www.clickandcompany.com, 1/26/21.
226. Photography interview with David duChemin. Clickin Moms Blog for Photographers. www.clickinmoms.com/blog/photography-interview-with-fine-art-photographer-david-duchemin/, 11/2/19.
227. LinkedIn message to the author, 8/2/19.
228. www.matiash.com/2014/11/19/four-photo-tips-improve-compositions/, 10/2/19
229. Photography interview with Jennifer Summer. Clickin Moms Blog for Photographers. www.clickinmoms.com/blog/interview-jennifer-summer/, 10/2/19.
230. Colton, Jim. Continued from Part One: Moments of the Human Condition. NPPA The Voice of Visual Journalists, 2017–2019. www.nppa.org/page/photo-journal-peter-turnley-part-2, 9/4/19.
231. Conversation with the author, Medium, Midwest Society for Photographic Education, Lexington, Kentucky, November 1–4, 2018.
232. Bond, Simon. 9 Tips for Aspiring Young Photographers. Digital Photography School. www.digital-photography-school.com/9-tips-aspiring-young-photographers/, 10/20/19.
233. Conversation with the author, Constructed Realities, Annual Conference, Society for Photographic Education, Las Vegas, Nevada, March 10–13, 2016.
234. Coleman, A. D. Piled Higher and Deeper. Photocritic International; A.D. Coleman on Photography and New Technology, 5/5/14. www.nearbycafe.com/artandphoto/photocritic/2014/05/05/piled-higher-and-deeper/, 10/28/19.
235. Keynote speech, Family Values, Society for Photographic Education, Annual Conference, Orlando, Florida, March 9-12.
236. Gilbert, Elizabeth. *Big Magic*. New York: Riverhead Books, 2015, pp. 123–124.
237. Email to the author, 9/14/19.
238. Meet Mickey Strand of Mickey Strand Photography. Local Stories, SDVoyager, 3/1/18. http://sdvoyager.com/interview/meet-mickey-strand-mickey-strand-photography-grantville-spring-valley/

Index

Made in the USA
Las Vegas, NV
01 November 2024

1b8c6d60-5139-4cbc-a1f7-b7e1d49e10f8R01